THE
Snow Globe

SEEING THE WORLD FROM GOD'S PERSPECTIVE

NICK PADOVANI
MO THOMAS
DYLAN DEMARSICO

Copyright © 2023 by Nick Padovani, Mo Thomas, and Dylan DeMarsico

The Snow Globe: Seeing the World From God's Perspective
by Nick Padovani, Mo Thomas, and Dylan DeMarsico

Illustrations by Carol Heiss

Designed & Published by Eyes Open Press
www.eyesopenpress.com

Printed in the United States of America
ISBN-13: 978-1-7360733-5-3 (paperback)
ISBN-13: 978-1-7360733-6-0 (e-book)

All rights reserved solely by the publisher. No part of this book may be reproduced in any form without the written permission of the publisher. The publisher does not assume responsibility for author or third-party websites and social media content.

Scriptures

Unless otherwise indicated, all Scripture quotations are taken from the *New American Standard Bible* (NASB95). Copyright © 1960, 1962, 1968, 1971, 1972, 1973, 1975, 1977, 1995 by The Lockman Foundation. Used by permission. All rights reserved.

Scripture quotations taken from the *Amplified Bible, Classic Edition* (AMPC). Copyright © 1954, 1958, 1962, 1964, 1965, 1987 by The Lockman Foundation. Used by permission. All rights reserved.

Scripture quotations taken from *The Holy Bible, English Standard Version* (ESV). Copyright © 2001 by Crossway, a publishing ministry of Good News Publishers. Used by permission. All rights reserved.

Scripture quotations marked (GNT) are from the *Good News Translation* in Today's English Version – Second Edition Copyright © 1992 by American Bible Society. Used by Permission. All rights reserved.

Scripture quotations taken from *The Message* (MSG). Copyright © 1993, 1994, 1995, 1996, 2000, 2001, 2002. Used by permission of NavPress Publishing Group.

Scripture quotations taken from the *New King James Version* (NKJV). Copyright © 1979, 1980, 1982 by Thomas Nelson, Inc. Used by permission. All rights reserved.

Scripture quotations taken from the *New Living Translation* (NLT). Copyright © 1996, 2004, 2015 by Tyndale House Foundation. Used by permission of Tyndale House Publishers Inc., Carol Stream, Illinois 60188. All rights reserved.

Scripture quotations marked TPT are taken from *The Passion Translation*. Copyright © 2017. Used by permission of Broadstreet Publishing Group, LLC, Racine, Wisconsin, USA. All rights reserved.

Scripture quotations taken from *The Voice* (VOICE). Copyright © 2008 by Ecclesia Bible Society. Used by permission. All rights reserved.

Contents

A Virgin Surrounded by Glass v

Part One: Harmony & Innocence 1
   I: The Fullness of Time 7
   II: The Tragedy 13
   III: The Great Entanglement 19
   IV: A Tale of Two Trees 25
   V: The Awareness of the Glory 33

Part Two: An Origin Story 37
   I: Pre-Beginning 41
   II: Creation 43
   III: Pandemonium 45
   IV: Entrance 47
   V: Projection 49
   VI: Division 53
   VII: Poison 55
   VIII: Invasion 59
   IX: Seed 63
   X: Crash 65
   XI: Finally 67

Part Three: Christ in Unsuspecting Places 73
   I: A Fall into Grace 75
   II: A Tale of Two Psalms 81
   III: The Circumcision of Christ 89
   IV: Seeing Christ Hidden in All 97
   V: Behold, the Riddle 105
   ...and in light of the above 110

The Authors & the Press 113

A Virgin Surrounded by Glass

"Come now, and let us reason together,"
  says the Lord,
"Though your sins are as scarlet,
They will be as white as snow;
Though they are red like crimson,
They will be like wool."
  ~ Isaiah 1:18

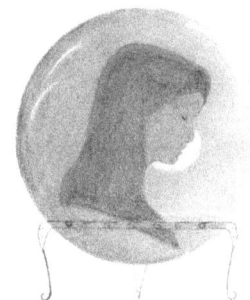

TRYING TO REASON YOUR WAY THROUGH LIFE is typically one of the most efficient ways to forfeit peace. Human reasoning—remarkable as it may be with its mysterious eruptions of billowing clouds of neurons racing along organic highways—is not the answer to life's greatest challenges and deepest questions. It can be wildly useful in our day-to-day happenings and necessary plannings, yet it cannot be the captain of the ship. These neural explosions are beautiful and strong, but they often amount to a puff of smoke in the face of the cosmic fire. The force necessary to blow through the veil of creation is just not there.

The ancient scriptures understood this limitation and accordingly give a call to lean not on our own reasoning abilities, but to embrace a life of abiding trust (Proverbs 3:5).

That said, there is one area the scriptures do call us to reason. Strangely enough, this has to do with the way we perceive the evil and darkness found in the world—and even in our own lives. It seems there is a place of reasoning where we can calculate a higher reality, one that supersedes the darkness we so often experience.

In this place we find the perspective of the Divine. Somehow, when God looks at the world, he beholds the pure and matchless image of his Son. He holds this whole world in his hands, as the song goes, and as he holds it, it is with the care of a joyful father tenderly holding a precious infant. Or, for this book's purpose, we could say that it is like a master artisan holding a treasured, handcrafted snow globe filled with white showers. Those showers are his very own glory, and they fill the entire globe.

We can take this metaphor a little further. Even if he shakes up this globe at times, allowing ancient boundaries to shift and chaotic forces to erupt, it is only with the purpose of spreading that snow of righteousness further and deeper. This shaking is then connected to the true meaning of the word "apocalypse," which many associate with horrific and bloody imagery. But we'll find this is another area where we need to adjust our "reasoning," for the word apocalypse simply means *unveiling*. The destiny of the cosmos is wrapped up in this unveiling of what God already knows to be true.

The Invitation Before You

Around the time we felt the call to write about these ideas, the image of a snow globe came in a dream. It was well after we decided to make this the title of the book that I decided to do some additional research on these ornamental objects. To my surprise, I discovered that the first snow globe ever made had a figurine of the Virgin Mary placed inside of it. I found this incredibly fitting when I thought about the theme and focus of this book.

The whole creation is much like the Virgin Mary . . .

It carries the hidden glory of Christ.

When Mary became divinely pregnant, there were many who passed her by and thought her to be an unfaithful woman. A "whore" was probably the word being secretly whispered throughout the community. This is partly why Joseph, being a godly man, wanted to quietly divorce Mary so as not to make a bigger spectacle of her (Matthew 1:19). But little did he know that the most pure and precious gift lay inside of her, a gift that transcended the "outward appearance" of Mary.

Inside of Mary's physical body was Christ himself. Behind the trillions of atoms that formed her flesh and blood was the growing seed of divine life.

The same goes for this entire creation. While many look at the world and see an aimless whore wandering through a sea of starlight (even "godly" people like Joseph make this same conclusion all the time), there is a greater and a more beautiful truth about this globe and its cosmic canopy. The growing seed of Christ is resident within.

This book is an invitation to come and reason together with our Creator and discover this glorious reality. Righteousness covers the world like snow shaken in wrappings of glass and silver. The crimson stain of sin has been washed away and replaced with the pure wool of the Lamb of God.

And there is even more to this . . . Just as Christ finally came forth from Mary's womb, the same holds true for the womb of our believing hearts and quieted souls.

In other words, God is going to shake everything that can be shaken, revealing the full righteousness of Christ that is already latent within creation. One day, the fullness of Christ will be unveiled throughout the entire world, which even now is pregnant with hope. But it is then that our own faith will become sight and our hope will become a surer reality (even though the reality was here all along).

It will finally come about that the unstoppable love of Christ will outshine everything else and we'll echo the words of Paul in his concluding thoughts about love in 1 Corinthians 13. Look at this carefully, for we will come back to this verse at the end of our journey:

> *Now we see things imperfectly, like puzzling reflections in a mirror, but then we will see everything with perfect clarity. All that I know now is partial and incomplete, but then I will know everything completely,* ***just as God now knows me completely.***
> *~ 1 Corinthians 13:12 (NLT)*

God knows the truth about us. He stares through the warbled glass of this globe and sees the completed work of his Son. Herein lies another layer to our metaphoric title. While we look at our lives and the world and so often see an imperfect and puzzling mess, God looks and beholds something much different. And the essence of the age-old term "repentance" is about aligning with this divine vision. It is about entering into the Creator's reasoning and discovering what he already knows to be true.

Such is the wild path we're about to walk down.

Part 1

Harmony & Innocence

Nick Padovani

"Look harder."
 ~ Rafiki

Not only that, but all the broken and dislocated pieces of the universe—people and things, animals and atoms—get properly fixed and fit together in vibrant harmonies, all because of his death, his blood that poured down from the cross.
  ~ *Colossians 1:20* (MSG)

And by Him to reconcile all things to Himself, by Him, whether things on earth or things in heaven, having made peace through the blood of His cross.
   ~ Colossians 1:20 (NKJV)

Through the Son, then, God decided to bring the whole universe back to himself. God made peace through his Son's blood on the cross and so brought back to himself all things, both on earth and in heaven.
   ~ Colossians 1:20 (GNT)

And through him God reconciled everything to himself. He made peace with everything in heaven and on earth by means of Christ's blood on the cross.
  ~ Colossians 1:20 (NLT)

And by the blood of his cross, everything in heaven and earth is brought back to himself—back to its original intent, restored to innocence again!
  ~ Colossians 1:20 (TPT)

I

The Fullness of Time

QUIETING THE SOUL IS ALWAYS AN EXERCISE OF TRUST. It requires your fingers to loosen their grip on the cliff of reason as you hang there with that constant desire to pull yourself onto some alluring solid ground where everything is figured out. But to find inner quiet is to let go of that pursuit and fall backward. Somehow, in that freefall, things come together and the most solid ground of peace is discovered. The wind at your back hits you like an old friend from your deepest and most cherished childhood memories. And all is well.

This can happen for a few seconds at a time, or it can extend into hours of peaceful reflection and awareness. But however long you embrace this inner quiet, you will always hear the same thing. Something undeniably beautiful.

You will hear the sound of harmony.

There is a deep harmony that runs underneath everything like a healing river winding in and out of the rocks of existence. This is a river that everyone walks through unaware, though we all consciously dip our foot into it from time to time. Some seek this river very intentionally; mystics and dreamers and the like. But each one of us is fully capable of encountering it. Sometimes it is in a moment of quiet by a fire or in looking up into a clear night sky. The harmony of everything sneaks up on you, refreshing your soul, and then seems to slink back behind the jagged rocks of life.

In all of this, there is another important exercise—the opening of the eyes of your heart. While quieting the soul is an exercise of faith, this one is more about hope; hope that reaches beyond our immediate vision in order to see something much deeper and truer.

If you can open your inner eyes long enough, looking intently at the world around you, you will see something else of unspeakable beauty.

You will see *innocence*.

A glorious innocence that permeates everything around us.

We catch glimpses of it here and there. Perhaps in a warm encounter with a dear friend, or at the sight of a new blossom in the spring, or even in a touching video that strikes your heart as you scroll through your social media feed. There is something pure in this world, something tangibly innocent that at the same time can feel utterly elusive and incredibly easy to lose sight of.

Throughout the Theater

Imagine something for a moment. Picture yourself standing in the back of a theater filled with a large group of people who are obnoxiously loud and engaged in all kinds of fruitless arguments. The strife can be seen in every direction and perhaps a fist fight or two breaks out here and there. One attendee has their fingers in their ears and is shouting randomly like a three-year-old. It's chaos.

But there's a stage at the front of the theater and upon the stage is that most talented and inspiring orchestra in the world. They are playing music so transcendent that it heals the heart and lifts the mind to a different place. But of course, you must tune into it.

Many people, too many of us, stay stuck in the chaotic noises. Even when we try to focus and listen to the music, we end up in arguments with the noisemakers, trying to reason with them or perhaps pray them away. But when we learn to just move closer to the orchestra, the other noises naturally fade. And soon enough the orchestra pulls us in without any own effort of our own, whereas at first the task seemed impossible. But as this pulling occurs, the problems throughout the theater become distant and trivial. Soon, the music engulfs your soul and all the past annoyances and problems are rendered meaningless.

Now imagine a similar theater. But instead of a stage at the front, there's a giant movie screen. Once again you're in the back, but instead of an annoying crowd of people, there are these different sized televisions set up on stands all over the place. Each TV set is playing something different, but all have this in common: The images upon them are distasteful. They are either boring or ill-made, or filled with vile images. And they are VHS quality with antenna-like reception.

But that movie screen at the front is smooth and crisp. Its technology is state-of-the-art and upon its tightly woven fabric plays a film of unimaginable beauty with a capturing storyline of epic stature.

If your eyes are fixed to the static in the smaller television screens, you'll miss the greater film in front of your eyes. But if you learn to focus in on the screen, its purity and message will overtake your heart and flood out the other screens.

The world around us is kind of like this. Quieting the soul and opening the heart are different ways to come in touch with the unspeakable beauty that surrounds us. A beauty can be summarized by these two painfully glorious words:

Harmony and innocence.

For those with eyes to see and ears to hear, these realities are everywhere. But there's a question we need to pose at this point:

Where does it come?

Where is the stage and screen?

Perhaps if we can find where this healing river is sourced, we can drink from it directly, instead of just dipping our foot into it from time to time, allowing it to haunt us with the allure of its touch. Perhaps there is a way to swim in its currents and discover new depths of its flow.

Bloody Headwaters

The answer to these questions is undoubtedly strange and extremely surprising.

It turns out that the stage is a tree and the orchestra is the beaten body of a Man hanging upon its limbs. The story playing out on the grand movie screen is the tale of the Gospel—an account of a Man from Nazareth who was lifted up and crucified for the corruption of the world.

The crucifixion of Jesus Christ is the headwater and origin of all the peace and purity that runs through creation. This was an event that happened 2000 years ago in time and space, but it came at a moment that the Scriptures call "the fullness of time" (Galatians 4:4). In that fullness, all of time and all of space was transcended and filled. The death of Christ affected everything everywhere and so became the source of everything's restoration. The cross is now the proverbial fountain of life that ancient conquistadors sought after and modern explorers still thirst for. It is a fountain that springs both water and blood, and it pours dignity, pureness, and tranquility back into the universe.

It is there that *all the broken and dislocated pieces of the universe—people and things, animals and atoms—get properly fixed and fit together in vibrant harmonies* (Colossians 1:20 MSG).

Or you could say that it is there that *everything in heaven and earth is brought back to himself—back to its original intent, restored to innocence again* (Colossians 1:20 TPT).

It wouldn't hurt to read those words a few times over… *Everything* gets properly fixed and put back together at the cross. *Everything* in heaven and earth is restored to its original intent. Somehow the symphony is playing again and the innocent loveliness of life is put back together, fully restored.

In other words, the cross is the place where Jesus released "righteousness" to the world. That's a word that sounds lofty and ethereal to some, but it can be boiled down into two simpler terms:

Innocence and harmony.

You might also call it "rightness." It is people and things (including animals and atoms) being *as they ought to be*.

This is what was released at the crucifixion of God.

Now perhaps the beauty of this Song and the power of this Film has not yet breached the other distractions around you. Don't give up. Keep tuning in . . .

II

The Tragedy

In the beginning, when the world was newborn, swaddled in the Spirit of grace, God carried it in his arms and called it "very good." He was acknowledging the essential innocence and peace throughout his creation. But obviously, something happened to this beautiful child. Something deeply unsettling. A perversion and twisting began to occur, like when you put your face in front of a carnival mirror and behold a contorted and warbled image of yourself. The creation was made to reflect the glory of God, and mankind was to be the clearest part of that image. But the reflection became "unrighteous." It became disharmonious and impure.

But herein lies another important question: *Is that original image gone forever?*

To this, I would suggest the following . . .

No . . . It was no more gone than your true face is gone when you look into a distorted mirror.

In fact, when you do that, your face is still perfectly intact. It's the reflection that's messed up.

The Creator and Sustainer of everything has continued to see the true face of his creation—including you and I. In reality, it was only our perception that got skewed. And a skewed perception led to skewed and twisted actions. But the glory was still there. In fact, it never left.

An Enemy in the Mind

Colossians 1:20 is a powerful verse filled with imaginable wonder. Let's look at it more closely:

> *And by Him to reconcile all things to Himself, by Him, whether things on earth or things in heaven, having made peace through the blood of His cross.*
> *~ Colossians 1:20* (NKJV)

Now keep reading and look closely at what comes right after that verse:

> *And you, who once were alienated and enemies **in your mind** by wicked works, yet now He has reconciled.*
> *~ Colossians 1:21* (NKJV)

We were enemies *in our minds*, the Scriptures say. It was our vision and perspective that became corrupted, and the "wicked works" went hand in hand with this false perspective.

The etymology of the word "wicked" is helpful to understand. It has to do with something being twisted out of shape. It has the same root meaning as the word "wicker" (as in the baskets and furniture made from the twisting of materials like wood or plastic). The idea is that there is something straight and solid there, but it has been warped out of shape. The original entity is intact, but it is bent, knotted, and gnarled.

The book of Genesis tells a story about Adam and Eve and how their "eyes" were opened at the Fall (Genesis 3:7). Many believe that this was more of a closing of the heart's eyes and an opening of the natural eyes where they would see and reason independently from God. They would no longer see according to God's word (including his perspective), but their own. This led to the embrace of a vision quite different from his.

It was at that moment that they realized they were naked, which ushered them into a consciousness that something was wrong. Guilt and shame flooded into the picture and, because of this, they began hiding from their Creator. Instead of staying in the place of rest and friendship (which is what *harmony* is all about), they now feared their Maker.

So, another question: After this introduction of guilt, did anything change outside of their perception?

Not at first.

The image and glory of their Father still dwelt within them. People might speculate that something tangible left them, but there is no direct statement about that in the creation story. The two of them were still surrounded by the glory of God. Plus, their Creator still loved them and continued to pursue them. This can be seen especially when God clothed the "rebellious" Adam and Eve with animal skins—a clear picture of the coming death of Christ who would re-clothe humanity with grace (see Genesis 3:21). More on this later.

From this moment, God continued to walk with humanity, even after they left the paradise of Eden (see Genesis 4). This proves that in truth they were not the enemies of God. But because of a twisted perspective and their ensuing "wicked works," they thought themselves to be enemies and walked according to this newfound identity. This meant acting like enemies, going so far as to destroy themselves and one another. Yet the truth remained the same: God's heart was still *for them*. Right from the beginning, he was even igniting a plan to resurrect the ashes of the original blessing that was upon humanity . . .

The original blessing of peace and harmony.

The Pressure and Power of Perception

Hopefully you're paying close attention to what's being said. This isn't a claim that the fall of mankind and the problem of sin is *only* a matter of the mind—as though everything is okay, we just need to change our intellectual thought processes. Things are obviously not okay at a very fundamental and even physical level. But the reasons for this do begin with the heart and mind. That is the central issue. For it is from the heart that the springs of life flow (Proverbs 4:23).

Our perception is so influential that it reaches out and affects the world around us, from our own bodies to the atoms that make them up. And this can certainly lead to a "curse" in the world around us.

Understand then that the curse of Genesis was not something God did to the world out of anger and retribution. He clearly said to mankind—fully represented by Adam and Eve—*"Because of you, the ground is cursed..."* (Genesis 3:17).

We cursed the ground, not God. This is because we are image-bearers of the Creator, and our own words and actions affect the creation around us.

Remarkably, all of this is something that scientific research is beginning to prove. Over the last century, the scientific community has made some spectacular discoveries that line up with this. The people who study the physics of the "very small" have done verifiable experiments that prove how our own observations of particles can affect their position and movement.

Pay close attention here ... Physicists have *proven* that our observation and focus can affect the fundamental pieces of matter and energy that make up the creation around us!

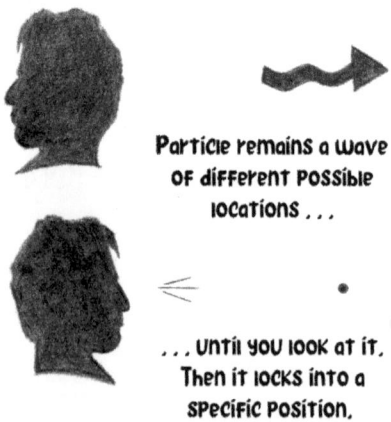

Particle remains a wave of different possible locations...

...until you look at it. Then it locks into a specific position.

Now of course, some people can take these scientific findings and go off into strange and varied teachings, taking it farther than the experiments imply. For our purposes here, it's the principle of the matter that we are concerned with. There are foundational principles of science that mirror greater realities. God designed this world in such a way that it can teach us things. Trees, butterflies, and sunrises teach us something about life just as much as they carry ecological purpose. This is because the universe declares the glory of God in a plethora of ways (Psalm 19:1).

In light of this, studying the fundamental particles that make up everything in creation can bring us a great deal of spiritual insight. This is why the branch of science known as quantum physics (the study of the very small) is especially intriguing, even to people who do not believe in the One who breathed these particles into existence.

So back to the point ... A human's observation literally affects the things that make up our universe. This holds many lessons for us, though there is one we're zeroing in on.

Our perception holds immense power.

And furthermore, our focus affects our reality.

The fall of man represented a titanic shift in perception. Interestingly enough, this shift began at a tree that was called the Tree of the Knowledge of Good and Evil (Genesis 2:17). The Hebrew word for "knowledge" can be specifically translated as *perception*. The "fall of man" was quite literally a moment of shifted knowledge and warped perception!

By eating from this tree, they no longer saw innocence, but mixture. They saw purity and evil. Harmony and disharmony.

They looked down at their own selves and judged their nakedness as evil, whereas before the thought hadn't even crossed their minds. Nonetheless, this one train of thought gave them a one-way ticket into fear and deception, affecting their lives and causing them to run and hide from God. This meant moving away from the very source of life, light, and wisdom, which brought new consequences and an even deeper twisting.

This change in perception was like a stone tossed into the waters of creation. It created a seemingly small splash, but the ripples went out from it and distorted the image of creation more and more. Eventually we no longer saw ourselves or God according to the truth. We no longer saw the original blessing that was upon us. This distorted reflection then led to a distortion of pure things like love, passion, and worship. All of a sudden, selfishness, uncontrolled emotion, and idolatry flooded the scene (see Romans 1:18-32). In our eyes, God became scary and our hearts became dark. And untold tragedy ensued.

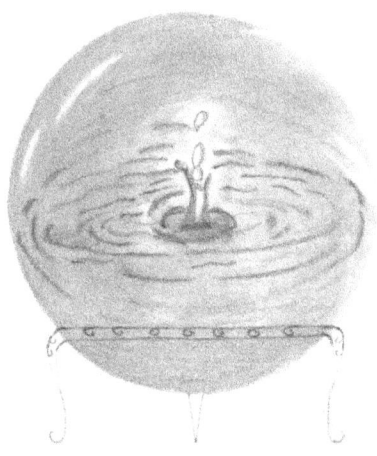

III

The Great Entanglement

Let's return once more to the centerpiece of our theater—the cross of Christ. We gave the strange and surprising claim that this was the redeeming source of creation's innocence and harmony. Now let's try and explain *why* that is.

We've looked at how the Tree of Knowledge brought the beginnings of distortion to the world. It is both poetic and providential that God would then use another tree to reverse this problem. At the tree of Calvary, Jesus Christ took on the disharmony and corruption of the *entire world* upon himself. His death was one that included all creation. This is a central part of the gospel, although many modern believers are unaware of the full scope of Christ's work.

Many believe that Jesus's death was an example to follow or an act that released an offer of forgiveness to some who would buy into it. While the gospel certainly includes these elements, it is far more holistic, all-consuming, and *cosmic*.

At the cross, the entirety of the fallen creation and its distorted imagery was united with the body of Jesus. *He became our distortion*. However, you might be more familiar with the phrase, *"He became sin"* (2 Corinthians 5:21).

The term "sin" originates from a Hebrew word that simply means to "miss the mark." It is the same thing as distortion or disharmony. So, Jesus took this sinfulness and gave us his righteousness. Again, the words "righteousness" and "sin" are synonymous with harmony and disharmony, innocence, and impurity.

A Light in the Darkness

Take a close look at the words of Athanasius, an ancient church father to whom we owe a great debt of gratitude. Among many other things, Athanasius stood against early attacks on the nature and identity of Christ. From day one, the system of this world vehemently came against the divinity of Jesus. Athanasius of Alexandria was a light in the darkness who helped both the eastern and western world become grounded in the truth that Jesus Christ *is God*, and that the Trinity is One entity. We'll get back to that in a moment, but for now, look at some of his teaching regarding Christ's work and its impact upon *all* creation:

> *The first fact that you must grasp is this:* **the renewal of creation has been wrought by the Self-same Word Who made it in the beginning.** *There is thus no inconsistency between creation and salvation for the One Father has employed the same Agent for both works, effecting the salvation of the world through the same Word who made it in the beginning.*
> ~ *Athanasius* ("On the Incarnation")

Creation has been *renewed* through the same Word Who made it. That's referring of course to Christ, who is called the Word of God (John 1). Through the cross, by Jesus's blood, everything is brought back to its original harmony. Everything is redeemed to innocence. This is because the corruption and its resulting guilt was fully placed upon the body of Christ at the tree of Calvary. This is a mystery that doesn't seem to make logical sense, but surprisingly there is a yet another scientific discovery that can give us some more understanding into this . . .

Further Quantum Insight

In the field of quantum physics, it has been shown that two particles can become mysteriously united to each other when they collide at high enough speeds. This is known as "quantum entanglement." Once this happens, the two particles will begin to mirror one another, even if they are separated by billions of miles of space.

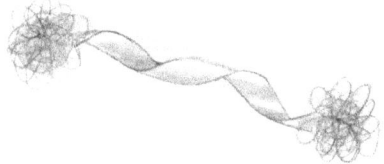

So, for instance, let's say two particles get "entangled" and you place one of them on the south pole of Neptune and the other one on a banana tree in Costa Rica. If you then go ahead and spin the one on Neptune in a certain direction, at the exact same moment, the one in Costa Rica will start spinning in the exact same way.

What baffles the minds of scientists to this day is the fact that all of this happens instantaneously. That means the particles are somehow communicating faster than the speed of light (it would take a beam of light about four hours to travel from Costa Rica to Neptune). Moving faster than the speed of light is impossible, so it's not like the particles are communicating to each other somehow. They are just *united* in some strange and unknown way. It's like an invisible string connects them no matter where they go.

Though the answers to this phenomenon haven't all come together, we understand that there is something that binds us together that is beyond the confines of space and time. Remember that we are looking at spiritual truths here. This mystery within the world of the very small has something to teach us about the heavenly truths we're unpacking . . .

Entangled with Christ

Jesus Christ came and entangled his physical body with creation. He collided into this world and became one with it through his incarnation—His act of being born into human flesh.

Now it's important to note that creation was already one with God because everything has always been sustained and held together in him (see Colossians 1:17). Jesus is the Word that formed and continues to uphold the entire universe (John 1:1 & Hebrews

1:3). Thus, *"in Him we live and move and have our being"* (Acts 17:28). We can never escape his presence because he pervades and fills all things (Psalm 139:7 & Ephesians 4:6).

Since Jesus remained fully God, even in his physical appearing, all of creation was still held within him. Even though he was fully human and located in one physical body, Jesus remained God and was thus completely omnipresent (which is why people who fought for the truth of Christ's divinity, such as Athanasius, are so important).

So what does this all mean?

It means that what happened to Jesus, happened to creation.

In him, creation itself was crucified and buried. We didn't see this happen, but it's a truth that transcends our physical senses. Jesus took on the full corruption of creation on his crucified body. Then when he died, the old order of things died with him. And thus, right at the moment of death, Jesus made a cosmically important statement:

> *Therefore when Jesus had received the sour wine, He said, "It is finished!" And He bowed His head and gave up His spirit.*
> *~ John 19:30*

Redemption was complete. Through the work of Christ, through the blood of the cross, the universe was restored to righteousness—completely. Having been cleansed through death, creation was then restored to innocence in Jesus's resurrected body, to which it was still entangled.

Really?

Of course, this all comes with some hard questions. This is a revelation that for some can be a very tough pill to swallow. The following is then a much-overused analogy, but it's too good to pass up: *The Matrix*.

You may know the scene. The main character in the movie is a man named Neo who is given the option of taking a blue pill or red pill. If he takes the red one, he'll be introduced to a world of truth beyond his imagination. Nothing will ever be the same for him. But if he chooses the blue pill, he'll wake up the next day and can go on with a "normal" life, accepting the world *as it appears*.

This revelation of the gospel—the full meaning of the crimson blood of Jesus—is like the red pill in *The Matrix*. It affects everything you thought you knew about creation, humanity, and the essence of Christianity. It absolutely changes how you see the world around you.

The revelation that all creation died and resurrected in Christ is tough to get down the throat for a number of reasons. First and foremost, it's tough because the world does not always look redeemed. "Innocence" and "harmony" are not exactly key words that people use to describe a good portion of the planet. From war to addiction to unbelief, it's hard to take the apostle Paul's words in Colossians seriously.

Because of this, many people will try to bend Paul's words toward an exclusive focus on the future. They will assert that Paul is describing the future day when everything will be outwardly restored to its original harmony. Or they might say that Paul is referring to *certain* things and *certain* people being "restored to innocence."

But that's not what the text is communicating.

Now you can take the blue pill and believe otherwise. But we're going to press on and go into even deeper waters. There is a false reality, *a matrix*, that is still covering people's eyes—including the eyes of many people who teach the Bible. But there is a way to see beyond this matrix and discover a new and redeemed world; to discover it, and then breath its air and set up camp on its shores.

Let's go there together.

IV

A Tale of Two Trees

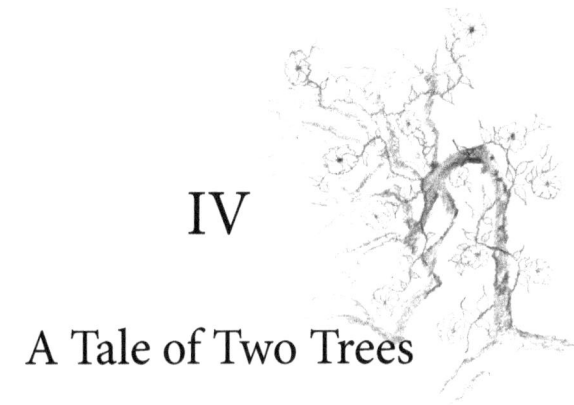

In the words of a wise monkey from another famous movie, each one of us needs to *"look harder."* This is what the old monkey Rafiki says in *The Lion King* to Simba as he stares into his reflection in the water.

Simba is a young lion riddled with guilt from his past who is living outside of his calling to reign as king. A scene comes where he stares into a pool of water and, at first glance, all he sees is the natural image—himself. He sees an image still muddled with shame and regret. But it is then that he is told to *look harder* until he sees the face of his father who lives within him. This is the one who reminds him of his true identity and his ultimate destiny.

What if there is a realm of seeing things in a totally different light? A realm that reaches beyond the distortion and discovers the identity and destiny of this creation and its inhabitants. *A realm of faith*, you might say. A place where we see the glory of our true Father in ourselves and in one another.

And what if this realm is more real than the one we naturally perceive?

The apostle Paul, the one who penned those majestic and weighty words of Colossians, wrote some other fascinating things regarding his perspective of people. Take a good hard look at how this great messenger of the gospel *perceived* the people around him:

> *Therefore from now on we recognize (perceive) no one according to the flesh; even though we have known Christ according to the flesh, yet now we know Him in this way no longer.*
> ~ *2 Corinthians 5:16 (parenthesis mine)*

Paul had come to a place where he no longer recognized *anyone* according to the flesh (or according to "outward appearances," as some translations render it). This comes just after Paul talks about a major conclusion he had come to in his life. *Look harder* at the famous verse that comes right before the one we just read:

> *For the love of Christ controls us, having concluded this, that one died for all, therefore all died; and He died for all, so that they who live might no longer live for themselves, but for Him who died and rose again on their behalf.*
> ~ *2 Corinthians 5:14-15*

Paul came to the realization that somehow *all had died*. Somehow, Christ's death included all people (and we've already discovered how it included creation itself). And so Paul, having come to this awakening of faith, writes the following:

> **Therefore** *from now on we recognize* **no one** *according to the flesh; even though we have known Christ according to the flesh, yet now we know Him in this way no longer.*
> ~ *2 Corinthians 5:16*

We have to see how verse 16 comes directly from the truths in verses 14 and 15. Paul had realized that all had died in Christ. *Therefore*, he recognized *no one* according to who they appeared to be on the outside. He had learned to look harder. And in doing so, greater truths began to trump the outward appearance of things.

Look Harder, Listen Closer

Here's the key in grasping this: We said earlier that the Tree of Knowledge released a lie, a shift in perspective that led to distorted actions and realities. The change in perspective was like a stone being thrown into creation that led to the ripples of outward corruption.

The Tree of Calvary did the same thing but in a reversed way. The cross was like an otherworldly stone thrown into the distorted waters of creation, which began to remove the ripples by releasing a new calm to the waters. The cross did all of this by revealing the truth of our forgiveness. It allowed us to look again at ourselves, knowing that we are now clean. We are as we ought to be—righteous—in God's eyes. Sin has been dealt with and the original truth about who we are is redeemed.

Moreover, the true face of our Father has also been re-revealed through Christ. Because of the cross, our minds are set free from seeing God as angry and fearful. Our Maker is not a destructive tyrant. He is perfect, sacrificial Love. He is a Love that casts out all fear of punishment (1 John 4:18). The cross heals our perspectives of the Creator, which is something that was lost at the first tree.

You see, the truth of this original image—our true image and God's true image—was always there. However, it became hidden behind the ripples of guilt, sin, and fear. Consequently, just like the first tree began with a lie believed in the heart, the second tree's de-rippling effect begins with a truth believed in the heart. Hence, the only way to swallow this red pill of truth is to enter through the door of belief. It begins with trust in the goodness of God (and the goodness of our forgiven self), which will extend out and purify our natural experiences.

In other words, once we start walking by this otherworldly faith, our actions will start to line up with its truth. Good works of righteousness will follow our awakened faith. If there is a lack of heavenly glory in our lives, it reveals that in some way our eyes are still closed and the heartbeat of faith is either slowed down or stopped. That's why the Scriptures constantly teach us to *grow in the faith*.

Paul knew all about this new world that was accessed by faith. He knew this faith involved seeing with a different set of eyes, which separated the false from the real (see Ephesians 1:18). This is about seeing beyond the immediate into a realm that is closer than we can possibly imagine. A realm of innocence and redemption…and hope. A Kingdom that is *already present* and alive for anyone with the eyes to see it.

> *… He answered them and said, "The kingdom of God does not come with observation; nor will they say, 'See here!' or 'See there!' For indeed, the kingdom of God is within you."*
> *~ Luke 17:20-21* **(NKJV)**

Eyes, Nature, and Mines

If you look hard enough, you can see a beautiful Kingdom inside of yourself, in others, and throughout the whole created order. You can especially see it when you look into the eyes of another human being. No matter how many tired cracks and wrinkles surround their gaze, and no matter how scowled or angry a person might appear, you can still discover this ancient glory **if you keep looking** according to the truth.

Furthermore—and this is so **important**—this vision of grace will change how you treat people. Otherworldly faith produces an otherworldly love where we actually treat others like we would treat Jesus Christ himself—because we actually *perceive* Jesus in others.

In some people and places, this original innocence and glory is much easier to spot. For instance, when you look at the smile of a precious baby your heart is instantly captured by its light. But when that baby grows up and encounters things in a world that is still held captive to lies (things that bring disappointment, regret, and doubt), the glory you once beheld gets hidden behind the crevices and scars of pain. But that *does not* mean the glory is gone. The original image is still there.

Nature is perhaps one of the easier ways to encounter the beauty of God in all its harmony and purity. People dip their foot into these waters all the time when they interact with a beloved pet or when they go on a hike and look up at the grandeur of a mountain range lit up by the sun. Whether with people, animals, or nature, there are countless moments and encounters where we can see and feel the undercurrents of innocence.

For the most part, however, we need to learn to *look harder*, because the glory is often hidden behind false distortions. Nevertheless, like a dirty mine, there is a treasury of precious diamonds for those who will search for the jewel of Christ hidden in all things.

Which, by the way, includes the dirty mines of our enemies.

Yes, if you look close enough into the face of a foe, their eyes might be glazed over by the internal battles of self-hate or the weariness of self-promotion, but you can still discover this treasure there as well. Traversing the dirt of this mine may take the tools of forgiveness and patience. It will certainly take an incredible focus of the heart's vision. But even still, the innocence is there, and finding it is like discovering a young child terrified and trembling behind a thick bush of thorns, thistles, and wasps.

Utter Disharmony

In my graduate studies, I took a class on domestic violence and child abuse where I learned and saw things that are very difficult to forget. One time I saw an image that had the potential to haunt me for a very long time; however, in the same moment I saw it, I was also given a glimpse of something from another realm. Something that changed what I saw and cleansed my vision.

The image was of a young teenage girl who had been hung against a pole in a basement with her arms suspended upward by ropes in a crucifix-like position. Before this, she had apparently been raped and abused by multiple people and was now hanging there to be mocked. She would soon die—and did in fact pass away.

Forgive the cruel imagery, but this gets at the very essence of *disharmony*. It is innocence absolutely mocked, destroyed, and torn apart. As a father of three precious girls, I can't even fathom such atrocity. This was a painful portrait of something absolutely wrong with our world. Something that makes the words of Colossians almost laughable. This is where we get to the nitty-gritty of our struggle with the gospel's truths.

This image penetrated my eyes like an intruder in my home, but in the same instance I was given a surprising gift from the Lord as a moment of clarity dawned upon my heart. I watched as the Lord began to wash the gates of my eyes with the same hand that I know will one day wipe away every tear from people's eyes.

At the same moment that I saw the girl hanging, I also saw the beautiful and beaten Christ hanging with her. I saw Jesus's own arms outstretched alongside hers as though he was taking the abuse upon himself. I caught a glimpse of something beyond the utter brutality of that event. It was Jesus suffering with this girl, embracing her, and holding her through it, taking on her pain, and then finally receiving her into his eternal realm.

Though I don't really have the words to express this, I began to understand how mercy would triumph over judgment (James 2:13). I saw somehow that the forgiveness of Christ and the power of his love would truly overshadow and overcome the sick and twisted distortions of this world. Somehow, I saw the blood of the Lamb overcoming the evil one and washing away all the wicked works produced through our deceived and alienated hearts.

Good, Evil, and Life

Let me try and explain this in a different way. It was as though the raw image of the hanging girl was a stark and sad visual of the Tree of the Knowledge of Good and Evil. On one side was goodness and purity—a beautiful young girl who did not deserve an ounce of what she had endured. On the other side was a jarring image of unspeakable abuse.

But in that moment of seeing Christ with her and in her, it was like God became a healing vine that wrapped his arms of love around her. The Tree of Knowledge was swallowed up by a Tree of Life. What at first was a scene of terror and repulsion, suddenly became a spring of hope as I saw this girl's innocence preserved and protected in Christ. I saw his love forgiving and overcoming the trauma of that event. I saw life triumphing over evil. And somehow my memory of this image was healed and *redeemed*.

None of the truths presented in this book are written flippantly or in ignorance of the evil and disharmony throughout the world. These are not the musings of a theologian sitting at a computer pontificating over nice Bible translations of an old apostle's words. This is a truth that goes deeper than the atomic structure of this universe.

There is a glory that fills this entire earth. Even right now. Even in the darkest and dirtiest of places.

Perhaps especially those places. For in the realm of hate, the light of love is exposed with all the more splendor. Though evil rears its ugly head, it is ultimately forced into the backdrop as love floods the scene with diamond-like brilliance. This is what the work of Christ accomplished and continues to reveal through the light of faith.

Eating and Drinking the Word

I am not asking you to understand all of this. What I am asking is that you consider partaking of it. You don't have to understand a type of food in order to partake and enjoy it. You don't need a clear explanation of the chemical make-up of pancakes and its interactions with the body in order to receive its goodness. In fact, if you overthink it, you might lose interest in the delicious meal in front of you. Or, at the very least, your meal will get cold while you're trying to figure it out.

All you need to do is just take a bite and receive it. And that is enough.

Take a bite of the gospel. Swallow the red pill. Look harder. And keep listening.

There is glory deep, deep in the earth.

V

The Awareness of the Glory

Ok, one last thing before I hand this off to Mo … A quick note about the word "gospel."

This word was handpicked by the Creator at a certain period in history to describe a particular message. As we learn to eat and drink of this message, it will be important to know that the original context of this word involved *the announcement of something*. The gospel was not a sales pitch. In its original setting, this term was used as a proclamation of a military victory that had already been accomplished. Hence, it's called **_good news_**.

In other words, the gospel is a glorious newsflash we are called to hear and trust in. It is in this trust where things get straightened out. Crooked ways become aligned. Valleys are raised high. Mountains are brought low. The "wicker" of evil is unraveled and restoration becomes visible. **The hope and vision of this book is to see this restoration come to earth just as it already exists in heaven. And it is to the people who carry this same yearning that we write these words.**

This understanding of the gospel's meaning should bring a new appreciation for the words the angels spoke when they announced the arrival of Jesus Christ. Speaking to shepherds keeping watch over their flock by night, a group of angels gave this wonderful announcement:

> *Glory to God in the highest,*
> *And on earth peace among men with whom He is pleased!*
>   *~ Luke 2:14*

God is *pleased* with mankind.

. . . He actually takes pleasure in this world.

Jesus's sacrifice is an eternal work that forever rises to heaven like the sweetest smelling incense carrying an intoxicating aroma. God himself is inebriated on the work of his Son, and he is overjoyed at each one of us as well, because we are all entangled with this same aroma of glory.

God is in a good mood!

The angels have always celebrated and looked forward to this. They look down upon the earth and see what God sees. In fact, here's a little line from one of their heavenly ballads. Hopefully, this will give you even more clarity on the matter:

> *Holy, holy, holy is the Lord God Almighty.*
> *The whole earth is **full** of His glory.*
>   *~ Isaiah 6:3*

In case you're wondering about the meaning of that bolded word "full"—it means exactly what it says. It's talking about *everything*. It's a word that means *complete*. The earth is *full* of his glory like the ocean is full of water. The two go hand in hand. In fact, the Hebrew of this verse could be translated as *"the fullness of the whole earth **is his glory**."* So, the earth is *his very glory*. They are entangled. They are one in the same.

And here's some even happier news . . . One day, the *knowledge* of this glory will fill the whole earth just like the waters cover the sea. (Again, because they are one and the same.) Instead of the knowledge of good and evil, the knowledge of Christ's cross and the glory of our oneness with God will fill the entire planet. Here's one of the Scriptures that declares this precious promise:

> *For the earth will be filled*
>   *With the knowledge of the glory of the Lord,*
>   *As the waters cover the sea.*
>   *~ Habakkuk 2:14*

And here is the same Scripture from another translation. Pay close attention to its wording:

> *For as the waters fill the sea,*
> *the earth will be filled with an awareness*
> *of the glory of the Lord.*
>   *~ Habakkuk 2:14* (NLT)

This translation gives a better understanding of the word for "knowledge" being used by Habakkuk. This word has to do with an "awareness" or "perception" of something. Therefore, God is promising to correct the distorted perceptions of humanity.

So keep in mind that this means the "glory" is already here. The promise is about humanity waking up to it again.

This is our great call. To awaken the nations. This book is written to the rising company of messengers who will go forth with fresh joy to stir a sleeping world out of its distorted bed. When we get to Dylan DeMarsico's section, we'll be empowered both with wisdom and practical guidance on how to step into this more directly.

In the meantime, we have a brief excursion before us—an excursion into deep time and into the sound that birthed the "Snow Globe" of our cosmos. Weaving his own journey of awakening with reflections on the story of creation, Mo Thomas will help set the stage for the joyful wake-up call we're invited to bring to others.

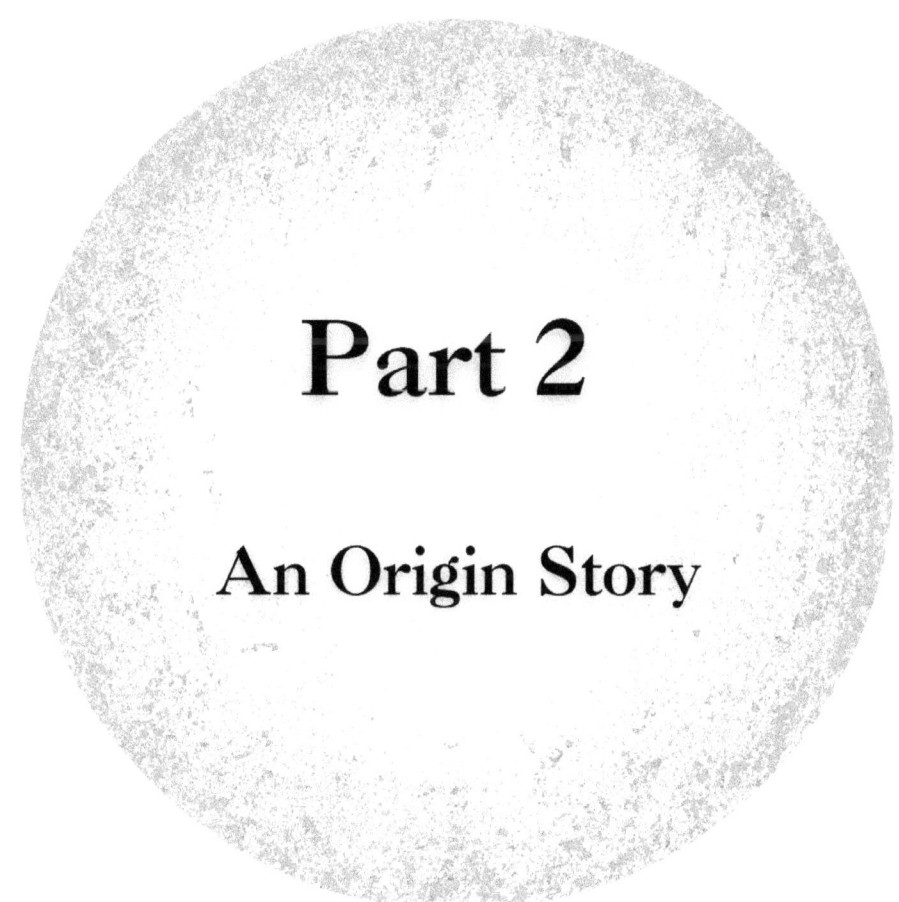

Part 2

An Origin Story

Mo Thomas

John 1 ~ The Voice
(A Snow Globe Paraphrase)

Before time itself was measured, the Voice was speaking.
The Voice was and is God.
This celestial Word remained ever present with the Creator;
His speech shaped the entire Snow Globe.
Immersed in the practice of creating,
all things that exist were birthed in Him.

His breath filled all things in the Snow Globe
with a living, breathing light—
A light that thrives in the depths of darkness,
blazes through murky bottoms.

It cannot and will not be quenched.

In the beginning, a Snow Globe graced existence—a captivating microcosm, lovingly crafted and nestled within its glass walls. Within this exquisite sphere lay the promise of a world both familiar and enigmatic, a reflection of the grandeur it held. Each delicate particle danced gracefully in the symphony of life, weaving an intricate tapestry that resonated through time. A masterpiece of divine artistry.

In this Snow Globe, I found echoes of my own story. Like the whirling flakes, my journey unfolded within its gentle confines. Unaware of the vastness beyond my limited perspective, I played my part in the intricate dance of existence. Yet, within the depths of my being, a yearning stirred, a hushed whisper urging me to venture beyond the boundaries of my self-made reality and uncover the hidden truths that lay concealed . . .

H O M E

Sometimes we forget that
we were born inside the heart of God

Even now
    our angst
  our self-loathing
  our restlessness and
    our deep doubts are all
      just reminders of "Home"

We can't feel "lost"
Unless we first "belonged"
We were born inside of Divine Love

Our lives are
       full of parables
            intended to nudge us
              toward the ultimate discovery
that underneath all of our surface "identities"
is our True Self • Uncreated and Utterly Magnificent

We must
     become aware of
what God sees as They gaze at us

I

Pre-Beginning

THIS IS NO ORDINARY SILENCE.

No. It is drenched with infinite possibilities.

This silence is terrifying and glorious and overwhelming.

It drips with the sheer magnificence of something that cannot, should not, be named.

What is this?!?!

It's been quiet for eternity. But something is different now.

Hushed anticipation. A collective held breath.

A Voice thunders in the darkness.

Light. Pure and Holy Light.

A Stunned Gasp.

Silence.

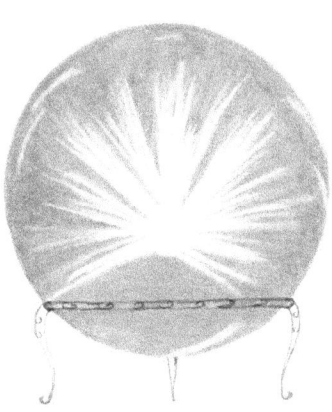

II

Creation

Within the Center of all things, the universe-to-be witnesses a cosmic explosion of Love, Joy, Freedom, Creativity, and Peace—an embodiment of Truth, Goodness, and Beauty. The Snow Globe of creation, encompassing both heaven and earth, takes shape deliberately and gradually. Expanding at an incomprehensible velocity, spreading out over 92 billion light years across, every particle within it is uniquely shaped and serves as a flawless mirror reflecting the ultimate reality at the Center.

In this realm, an overwhelming sense of awe and wonder prevails. All existence originates from a minuscule dot, what modern science calls a Singularity, the focal point from which the entire universe begins to form. This origin points us to what the scriptures refer to as *Christ*:

> *"[Now] He is the exact likeness of the unseen God [the visible representation of the invisible]; He is the Firstborn of all creation. For it was in Him that all things were created, in heaven and on earth, things seen and things unseen, whether thrones, dominions, rulers, or authorities; all things were created and exist through Him [by His service, intervention] and in and for Him. And He Himself existed before all things, and in Him all things consist (cohere, are held together)."*
> ~ ***Colossians 1:15-17*** **(AMPC)**

As the Snow Globe takes shape, sustained by the Source of All—the Spirit of Light, Love, and Laughter—its intricate splendor flourishes. Each particle is carefully aligned to face the Center, each one uniquely reflecting the Pure Light of Being when at its designated angle. Photons of light dance effortlessly among them, weaving together in a symphony of colors—an awe-inspiring kaleidoscope of a hundred trillion hues. This multidimensional mural showcases the full radiance of the sustaining Reality, an orchestrated harmony of swirling worlds colliding with order and grace.

The entire realm is connected, each part perfectly and precisely reflected, presenting a cosmic exhibition of a Divine Dream brought to life. Amidst this breathtaking scenery, one mirror-particle stands apart—a tiny, meticulously crafted sculpture composed of particles from across creation, infused with Divine breath. It is the purest and most captivating reflection of the Source.

This particle, known as "Adam," symbolizes all of humanity, serving as the reference point for all others. It exists to fully embody the perfectly reflected image of Divine Light and Love. The Snow Globe now stands as an ecosystem suitable for the manifestation of Truth, Goodness, and Beauty.

Yet, a dark and deceitful dagger was about to descend.

III

Pandemonium

Drawn by a persuasive and deadly deception, the Adam-particle drifts toward the edge of the Snow Globe, lured by forbidden fruit and the promise of meaning, satisfaction, and identity outside its Divine Community of Love.

The desperate cries of the entire Globe echo, pleading, *"Why? Why seek elsewhere when everything within this realm was created for you? All for you!"*

Yet, the deep longing for external validation creates a small opening through which a lie infiltrates. This lie distorts everything, accompanied by whispers of separation from the Divine . . . humanity runs away and hides because they are afraid, ashamed, and see themselves as guilty, worthless sinners at the very core. Despite the Globe being filled only with Goodness, an inner craving emerges for something else, something different, as if God's provision were not enough.

This deception is not isolated. The entire creation knows how swiftly this lie will spread, how deeply it will penetrate, and how profoundly it will distort our collective perceptions of reality.

Violent tremors shake everything, and an eerie darkness descends, replacing the clear atmosphere with a thick, oozing oil-like substance. The floating fragments transform into twisted, cloudy darkness. Each mirror-particle is knocked off its axis, no longer facing the Center. Instead, they begin reflecting the twisted misrepresentations of neighboring particles, assimilating the skewed images surrounding them. Gradually, a new world takes shape—a realm teeming with tiny funhouse mirrors displaying dangerous distortions.

The Snow Globe hurtles toward disaster, invaded by these deceptive illusions. The once-clear glass is now clouded with the dark residue of fear, shame, and insecurity. Muddied mirrors reflect back fragments of our identity, creating false labels and shallow personas.

However, despite the apparent trajectory toward turmoil and terror, the Reality at the Center remains tranquil. Beneath the clamor and chaos lays a sense of hushed anticipation and unshakable certainty.

The Story within time and space has only just begun.

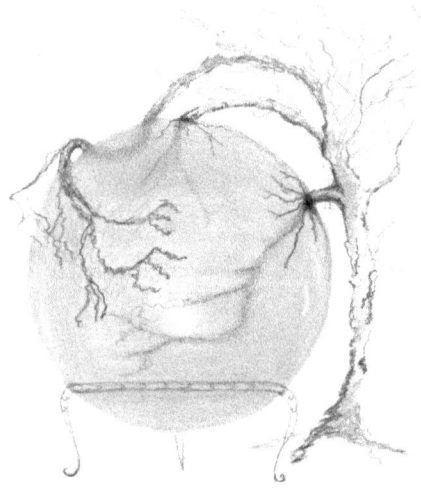

IV

Entrance

I was born into the Globe as an original manifestation of Truth, Goodness, and Beauty—a Love-Child of the Light. Overflowing with Love, Joy, Freedom, Creativity, and Peace, I had the capacity to flood the entire planet. Although I was too young to comprehend this truth, its resonance echoed faintly in the depths of my spirit. Words from an ancient text I had memorized as a child seemed appropriate:

> *You see all things; nothing about me was hidden from You as I took shape in secret, carefully crafted in the heart of the earth before I was born from its womb."*
> *~ Psalm 139:15* (The Voice)

I remained unaware of the stunning implications of all this, yet the Reality persisted, uncontainable and powerful.

The center of my own being was joined to the Center of all things (1 Corinthians 6:17), and the radiance of this Reality permeated the far reaches of the Cosmos, touching all it encountered. In my youthful naivety and exuberance, I stood resilient against the Lie, living authentically according to the Truth.

I embodied the Pure Light of Being, a unique Expression of Love in a package called Me.

I existed as this Divine-Expression-Called-Me before the world attempted to influence me; manipulating, convincing, and threatening me with its distorted reflections that transformed into labels . . . deceptive funhouse mirror images that masqueraded as my truth. These labels and lies nearly drove me to the edge, becoming an integral part of my existence. They subtly and subliminally attached themselves to me over time, reinforced by numerous people and influences, until they felt like an inseparable aspect of my identity. They got stuck deep within my heart and mind, adhering with the insidious substance of self-deception, and eventually, I questioned whether these labels could ever be stripped away.

But let's not rush ahead too quickly in the Story.

This was before all that, when I first entered the Globe as a Love-child of the Light.

Stay rooted in this moment! Be present. Breathe deeply. Remember.

Pure Light of Being. A unique expression of Love in a package called Me.

I Am.

Here I come.

V

Projection

During my junior high years, I encountered a lie—one that I have carried with me for most of my life. Despite the passage of many decades, its weight has persisted, silently casting its deadly spell.

"What will anyone ever see in Mo?"

At first, these words seemed insignificant, uttered by a cocky classmate in a school hallway, completely unaware of my presence. I tried to ignore it, laughing it off as I proceeded to my next class. Yet, this seemingly harmless sentence snarled malevolently and slithered within me. It plunged deep, implanting itself in the soil of my soul, and from that day forward, it began to grow. Its roots spread throughout my being, infiltrating every aspect of my thoughts, emotions, perceptions, beliefs, and experiences.

As this little lie made its home within me, it extended invitations to similar falsehoods in the world, strengthening its hold over me. I was oblivious as the funhouse mirrors surrounding me perpetuated these lies and labels in my subconscious mind, insidiously shaping my life without my consent or awareness.

I became ensnared in a web of parallel, subliminal lies: I would never be enough, I lacked what it took to measure up, and I needed to change to be accepted by others. I grew increasingly insecure in my own skin and had to find ways to hide my own shame.

Then, I discovered what seemed to work: performance. Subconsciously, I believed that my achievements could make up for my lack of self-confidence. And so, I devoted myself entirely to this pursuit. I gave it my all.

We all harbor hidden lies in our subconscious mind-programming that feed on our fears, our insecurities, our guilt and our shame, which cause us to employ covert coping mechanisms to navigate our lives. This plays out differently for each of us based on our unique experiences since birth, as our lives are carried along by a torrent of subconscious memories that avoid our awareness. For me, I tried to define myself through my performance. This was my coping mechanism, my addiction. It didn't matter whether it was sports, academics, music, behavior, or friendships—I was determined to be the best. I couldn't allow that cocky kid's words to prove true.

Valedictorian, class president, blue ribbons, trophies, MVP titles—I pursued them all relentlessly. I had to win, be first, excel, and gain the approval of others. I became a high-performance people-pleaser in response to that junior-high lie and its myriad deceptive companions. These achievements became my shield against the pervasive insecurity and shame that colored every part of my being.

Addictions come in various forms, not always limited to drugs, alcohol, food, or pleasure. They start to form whenever we start reaching externally for anything we perceive is going to fill the void inside us. My addiction manifested as a combination of performance and people-pleasing, resulting in a slow and deadly draining of my soul that lasted for many decades.

To others, it appeared as though I was thriving, living the epitome of the Good Life. At certain times, it felt that way to me too. Those around me validated my performance and achievements, which of course felt like they were validating me. Wasn't this the abundant life I was promised in Sunday School? However, they weren't validating the real Me. They were validating the projected versions of Me. I amassed a collection of hollow, flowery, fake affirmations and wore various convincing masks to evade confronting the insecurity that drove me. I was ashamed of myself and didn't realize it.

I mastered the art of projecting different personas tailored for each situation, adept at being whoever others needed me to be. So proficient, in fact, that I lost sight of my true self amid the confusion of my projected avatar. The unique Expression of Love encapsulated within me remained hidden and unseen. Beneath all my achievements, beneath the thin veneer of external validation, lay a frightened and insecure child, awkward and ashamed, horrified by the thought of being exposed.

So, I walked my life path cautiously, conveying a carefully constructed image to the world. I sacrificed authenticity, molding my persona to fit the expectations and judgments of others. I broadcast various versions of myself that I knew would be accepted and applauded. Yet, deep down, I knew the hollowness of this mind game, the emptiness that accompanied my striving for external validation. The masks I wore grew heavy, concealing the essence of who I truly was.

When we trace our family lineage far enough back, we discover that seeking external validation as a substitute for our God-given internal reality has been a convincing deception since the very beginning.

VI

Division

Within the depths of my being, a toxic brew of self-doubt, worthlessness, and shame was bubbling and spreading. It infected every facet of my existence, distorting my perception of self as well as the world around me. I became convinced that I was irredeemably flawed and unholy at my core (so was everyone else), which meant that we were all separated from God and each other.

I was told that if I wore a "Jesus" coat, God would overlook my unholiness and only see the perfection of the Son of God. Unfortunately, this message didn't affect the "me" hiding underneath this coat, and simply reinforced my underlying fear and shame. Because I was part of a religious system with authority figures that taught with great certainty about these matters, I was convinced of my status as an insider within this system, as long as I wore this "coat." I learned to articulate my insider beliefs beautifully . . . but beneath all the words was a profound emptiness, and an even more profound lack of authenticity.

In our journey through life, we have a tendency to gravitate toward those who share our ways of seeing the world. It provides us with a sense of security and safety to surround ourselves with individuals who reinforce our beliefs, no matter how flawed or false they may be. We seek validation and confirmation from others, even if it means perpetuating the illusions we have constructed within ourselves. This shared reinforcement solidifies our divisions and separations, cementing the false identities we have adopted.

As a result, we form factions and groups based on countless parameters that separate us—religion, politics, race, economic status, nationality, and so many more. Instead of recognizing the magnificent unifying Love that intertwines us from the very beginning of our collective Story, we fixate on the differences and distortions that divide us. These twisted mirrors that surround us create the twisted labels we assign to ourselves and others, which then contribute to the violence, conflict, wars, addictions, and disharmony that plague our world today.

When we gather in our respective factions, we create echo chambers where our shared distortions are amplified and reinforced. We find solace in the familiarity of our exclusive perspectives, finding temporary refuge from the discomfort of confronting the possibility that "our group" may not have the complete understanding of all truth. As we double down on the certainty of our own beliefs, we become further entrenched in our separateness, oblivious to the inherent unity and interconnectedness that underlies our existence. This is a brilliant mechanism designed to prevent widespread recognition of the glorious union woven through the tapestry of our collective Story.

This was me, in my religious echo chamber, surrounded by mirrors that reinforced my own toxic beliefs.

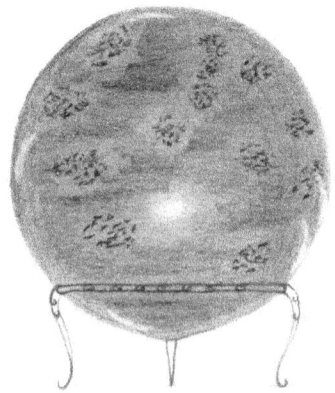

VII

Poison

Under the radar of my conscious awareness, I had ingested a persistent and poisonous lie, one that shaped the world I experienced, thought about, and perceived. I believed I saw the world as it truly was, unbiased and unfiltered, but in reality, I saw the world as I was—infected to the point of being unable to recognize my desperate need for help, hope, and healing. Bound by the poison's grip, I gravitated toward those who shared my distorted perspectives, further distancing myself from finding my True Self.

I yearned for purpose, meaning, and substance. I desired to know who I truly was, although at the time, I thought I wanted more tangible and socially acceptable external things. I hadn't yet discovered what I truly needed.

Occasionally, a phrase would whisper softly in the corridors of my soul, resonating deep within me: "A unique Expression of Love in a package called Me." It sounded powerful and inspiring, something that could adorn a bumper sticker. It was just that I had no idea what do with it! I didn't have time for smooth spiritual sales pitches or clever mind games. I craved straightforward, honest answers.

Who am I? Who can I turn to for guidance and who can I trust? I believed I should seek answers from God, but I gradually became aware that my understanding of the Divine had been severely distorted as well.

Eventually, I discovered that the "God" they had taught me about in my childhood was just as skewed as the creation around me, worsened by the projection of my own fears, insecurities, and shame. I had projected my own inner distortions onto the Divine, fashioning an image mirroring my darkest shadows—the parts infected by the poison, the lie.

Ironically, I became terrified of this deity I had crafted in my head, fearing I could never measure up to the set of holy standards imposed upon me. The notion of eternal torment in hell haunted my young heart, a fear-inducing tactic employed by religion. This blatant fearmongering should never have deceived anyone, but it has captured countless individuals throughout history because it has been sold as a God-sanctioned and biblically-mandated necessity tied to his holiness and justice. And this "necessary" punishment did not come with the possibility of correction or repentance; rather, it was a terrible scene of endless, gratuitous violence and horror . . . which served as an effective threat to control the masses.

Over the course of my life, I had mind-created a deity I called "God" without realizing the consequences. As those around me reinforced and affirmed the same projected image, it became the only "truth" I knew. This is how it works! When enough people repeatedly assert the same thing in various creative ways, false projections seem like reality, and lies appear true. I believed my projected god was the Real God. Naturally, I had no knowledge of any difference, and most people remain unaware that the god they imagine in their own minds, a god who aligns solely with their beliefs and rejects all others, is not the God who is the Source of All Things.

This deception is profound. We have fashioned a god from the palette of our shadow selves, justified it by using our sacred scriptures, and then weaponized this deity to enforce "appropriate" behavior. Meanwhile, Love and Light struggle to penetrate the depths and illuminate the original beauty of our Divine-Image-Bearing humanity. There is an immense disparity between the world the Real God envisioned, and the world we have constructed from the collective collage of our darkened imaginations.

Over the following years, many things that had provided me with security and confidence began to shift. The entire Snow Globe of my life started shaking violently, leaving nothing in its original place. The "Good Life" I had embraced since my youth slipped from my grasp. Due to my misguided notions about God, I began to blame him for not meeting my expectations. I oscillated between guilt, shame, and apathy until the burden

I carried became unbearable.

I found myself at the entrance of a new journey. The familiar world I had known collided with the possibility of something more—a realm beyond the veils of perception. A very dim and tangled path unfolded before me in the darkness, beckoning me to step into the unknown, to venture into the uncharted territories of my being. It was a call to awaken, to release the grip of illusions and embrace the truth that lay dormant within.

VIII

Invasion

The journey toward rediscovering our true selves and dismantling the barriers that divide us requires a collective awakening. Together, we must confront the shared distortions that have seeped into every aspect of our lives, understanding how they foster a sense of separation. By embracing our common humanity and challenging the twisted narratives that fuel division, we can begin to untangle the web of illusions ensnaring us.

Only through a shift in consciousness—choosing love over fear and unity over division—can we rise beyond the constraints imposed by our distorted perceptions. Embracing our authentic selves and peeling away the layers of falsehood become paramount to reclaiming our connection and contributing to the harmony and wholeness of our world.

One night as I lay in bed, on the precipice of sleep, an unexpected encounter unfolded within me. From the depths of my being, I felt a divine Light penetrate my very skin, piercing through the masks, covers, and false affirmations, reaching my core. In the middle of my desperation, the saltwater of my tears mixed with the blood-stained testimony of my broken heart. This Light crashed through the entire mess, and soon, the rushing of Living Water echoed within me like the roar of a raging river.

In that moment, I longed to redirect the furious flow of Light-bathed water toward the distorted images of fear, shame, insecurity, and darkness. I yearned to proclaim the truth, to expose the pitiful, persistent, and poisonous lie that had infected everything and everyone. *If I could shout loudly enough, persistently enough, would it be enough? Would I be enough??*

There was an underlying feeling beneath all my emotions—an ethereal whisper of hope and healing.

Over the years, subtle hints had penetrated my mind and heart on occasion, suggesting that the labels I had worn throughout my life, the core beliefs that shaped my existence, were not real. Perhaps the mirrors surrounding me had not been conveying the complete truth. Maybe there was something more profound, truer than my thoughts and feelings. Something magnificent, capable of tearing away all that was not True, Good, and Beautiful, leaving behind only what was Real. And when these hints touched me, an indescribable feeling surged through my being.

Do you recall those labels, the ones formed by the funhouse mirrors that clung to my heart with that unearthly adhesive called "self-deception"? I felt a surge of euphoria, akin to the adrenaline rush of a heart-pounding thrill ride, coursing through my entire being, ushering in a profound freedom. It was as if a heavenly elixir flowed from the depths of my soul, targeting those heart-labels with surgical precision, peeling them away and healing the wounds they left behind.

That shaft of Light, emerging from the very origin of creation itself, was working a beautiful transformation within me—I could feel it.

The initial removal of labels proved the most painful. Those early deceptions gave birth to the most persistent labels and were the hardest to uncover. Once I became aware of these sticky lies and managed to tear off the first few, sizable fragments of my heart felt like they were being ripped away with them.

During this intense pain, I felt the shaft of Light piercing through to my very essence, illuminating those labels for what they truly were: lies, poison, distortions, limiting beliefs. These deceptions were the insidious fruit growing from the soil of separation, exclusion, shame, fear, and darkness. This beam of Pure and Holy Light exposed the funhouse mirrors all around me, the ones that reinforced my false identity-labels, preventing me from unveiling the unique package called "Me" and embracing its fullness.

The joy, freedom, and exhilaration of our True and Authentic Selves have existed in seed form since the very beginning. The poison sought to conquer it, assaulting it from every angle, attempting to suppress its destiny. Yet, the seed remained untouched and untarnished, protected by the Divine from all interference.

And the seed was nurtured. Most of its growth occurred beneath the surface, as roots delved deeper with every passing moment, even amidst the chaos that I thought would consume me. As the false labels were ripped away, leaving behind a bloody mess, my tears flowed endlessly, serving as liquid prayers watering the seed deep within me.

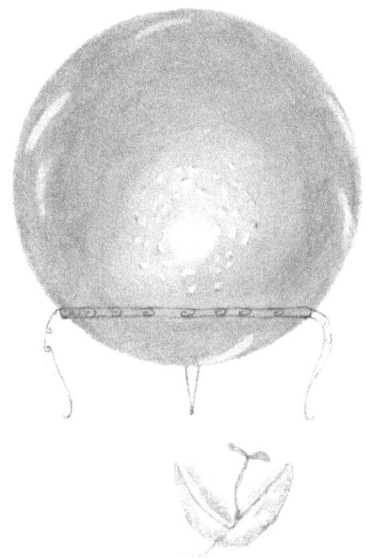

IX

Seed

A strange thought, like a slow train crossing through my mind, appeared.

Within the depths of my being, there is a sacred seed untouched by this poison.

What lay within that seed? Maybe, just maybe, it was infinite possibility, a way of living free from the shame and fear that had shaped my world. Maybe it held the key to uncovering my true identity and experiencing transformation.

The journey toward that seed was not easy. I had become so accustomed to the labels and projections that surrounded me, reinforcing my false identity. They screamed at me, persuading me that I would never be enough. And I believed them. The army of lies and labels grew strong, and fear kept me hiding in the dark, pushing me further and further from my true self. It was difficult to trust what I might find deep inside. The noise of the world drowned out the whispers, and doubt clouded my perception. I questioned if I could truly uncover the magic within me.

In a moment of great foolishness, or maybe it was a burst of wisdom, I placed a profound possibility on the table . . . I acknowledged that the path to transformation might require everything to fall apart. It was a daunting realization, but I understood what was necessary to dismantle the false persona I had constructed. Whispers from an ancient language echoed in my soul, reminding me of something greater, something beyond the noise and distractions. They urged me to listen, to embrace the hope that resided within me. I knew deep within that this seed held the power to change everything, to bridge the gap between who I had become and who I truly was.

Yes, it began with those wordless whispers, reaching the depths of my being and fortifying my heart for the horrors to come.

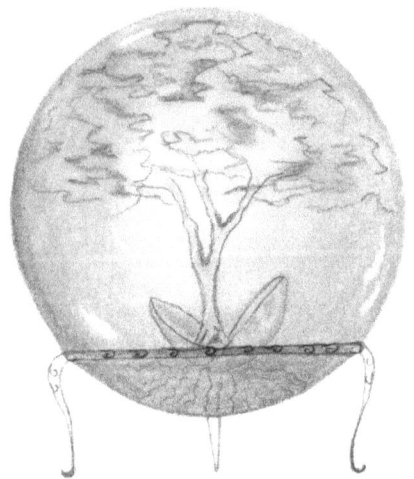

X

Crash

And so, it all came crashing down. I sacrificed my façade, dismantling the foundations of my identity. It was a journey of devastation, a series of breaking points that shattered everything I had clung to for my sense of self. The crash was a gradual unraveling, a dismantling that felt like eternity. Everything fell away, leaving me in ruins, unsure of who I was. It truly felt as though I was in hell.

The world around me had to crumble before I could see the truth. Others may find this awareness through different means—a heavenly display of love or a moment of deep grace. Whatever the catalyst, it requires an opening, a vulnerable softening of the heart, to recognize the lies we have internalized.

For me, with each devastation, with each shattering of an illusion, I moved closer to the sacred seed within me. It beckoned me toward a deeper understanding of my true self, and a profound eternal connection with God and the whole creation. Limitless possibilities were waiting, free from the shackles of false beliefs and fears.

I started from scratch, asking for a do-over, separating myself from the thoughts, feelings, and beliefs that had defined me. It was a humbling process, erasing the inner whiteboard and starting with a blank canvas. Resting, healing, unlearning, and unbecoming became my journey, guided by a multitude of beautiful clues from the universe. As my outer world crashed, my inner world crumbled also . . . and the rebuilding process began.

The journey was far from easy, but I knew it was the only way to reclaim my authenticity and embark on a new path of growth and wholeness. I trembled at the thought of what I might discover within its depths. This trembling was part terror, part exhilaration.

Perhaps there was a realm before I was filled with subconscious conditioning—the vibrations, words, and feelings I had absorbed since birth. What was imprinted on our souls when we arrived into the world? Was our inner whiteboard blank at the very beginning? Maybe we were filled with magical and magnificent mysteries written in an ancient, wordless language.

I gave the Holy Artist full permission to paint portraits on my soul, breathtaking images that expressed the truth of who I was created to be. As Spirit started painting, I realized that the "new" images were hints of images already within me, resonating deeply as reminders of my Highest Self. The seed, the core of my being, held those original images, my reference point that had been established before the foundations of the earth. As I saw these inner portraits taking shape, I began to experience them in my depths, as if for the first time. I was overcome with awe and emotion.

In the words of Peter, I had been reborn from eternal seed through the enduring word of God. The Psalmist expressed this awe and gratitude for being fearfully and wonderfully made, a unique expression of Divine Love. And from the story in Genesis, Divine Spirit had joined with the dust of the ground to become Me (Genesis 2:7).

The part of Me that is connected to everything and everyone, including the Divine, *knew that it knew* that this seed had not *just* been deposited into Me, but into *every single person in the universe*. And my experience was going to end up becoming a bridge for others to experience in their deepest being, a transformation that allowed them to become who they truly are . . . A divine image-bearer that God saw and loved before time even existed.

XI

Finally

And so it happened, just as it had to. The foundation crumbled, my external labels and achievements shattered. I no longer recognized myself without them. It was a necessary destruction, making space for something new to emerge. It was a glorious breaking, shaking, and shattering.

In the aftermath of my life's wreckage, a great silence descended. The silence was pregnant with possibility, beckoning me to listen. In that quietude, I began to hear the whispers of my soul, the ancient language of Love.

Deep down, I had always known. My inner "knower" was fully aware. Every moment in my life had led me to this pivotal point. The Seed within me had to bring forth its Life.

I remembered that the Kingdom of Heaven is not some distant place, but a reality invading the earth. The knowledge of the glory of the Lord is destined to fill the earth as the waters cover the sea (Isaiah 11:9).

Within the original Sacred Seed resides all that is True, Good, and Beautiful. It holds the potential to grow into a mighty tree, offering healing and nourishment to the nations.

Then, thunderously, the Voice speaks . . . this time, from within my spirit. Pure and Holy Light explodes, illuminating every corner of my being.

Finally, I can see.

In the Snow Globe of my life, I discovered the truth—that the entire universe exists within the confines of my being, waiting to be unveiled. As I set aside the noise and illusions, the original Sacred Seed began to blossom into its full potential. As a result of this awakening, I can respond to the invitation to live authentically and radiate the transformative power of Love to the world.

I now refuse to let fear, shame, and guilt shape my life through persuasive, false labels. With newfound clarity, I see the limitations of masks and the futility of seeking validation outside myself. What I've sought out there throughout my existence has always resided within me. My inner world mirrored the world outside, and I realized that the true journey lay in discovering the Pure Light of Being that shines within. The distortions and deceptions that had shaped my existence no longer hold sway.

I embody the Pure Light of Being, a unique expression of Love in a package called Me.

SELAH

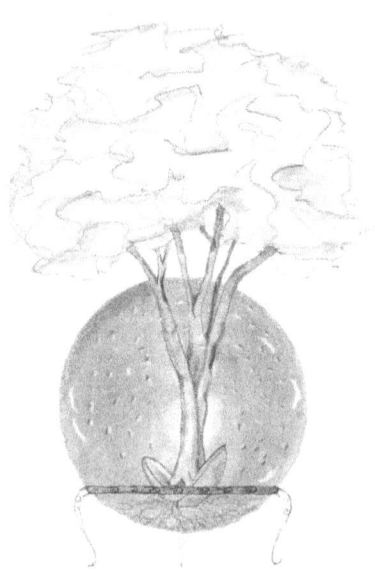

DISTORTIONS

Have you ever looked in a mirror
  And looked at yourself the same way
    That God sees & feels about you right now?

The Real You lies underneath
  All the distortions you've seen
    In the fun house mirrors that you
      Thought were your real reflection

Fake Mirrors were reinforcing your False Self

God alone knows the Truth about you
    You might be . . . FAR MORE Beautiful
      Than you've ever known was possible

Ask Them to
  Show you who
    You Really Are

Then wait . . . in the Silence
  Until the Reality of your Being
    Whispers from your deep spirit
      And persuades you of the Truth

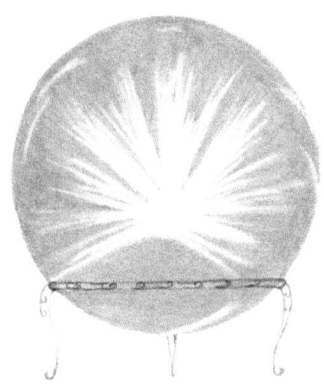

Revelation 21 ~ The Voice
(A Snow Globe Paraphrase)

And I heard a great voice, coming from the throne.

A Voice: *See, the home of God is with His people.*
He will live among them in the Snow Globe;
They will be His people,
And God Himself will be with them.
The prophecies are fulfilled:
He will wipe away every tear from their eyes.
Death will be no more;
Mourning no more, crying no more, pain no more,
For the first things have gone away.

And the One who sat on the throne announced to His creation,

The One: *See, I am making the entire Snow Globe new. (turning to me)*
Write what you hear and see, for these words are faithful and true. It is done!
I am the Alpha and the Omega, the beginning and the end. I will see to it that
the thirsty drink freely from the fountain of the water of life.

COSMIC SNOW GLOBE

I don't want to stray
Yet I know I can't stay
Within the walls of
Theological structures
That attempt to
Constrain Reality.

I was taught
The God of Religion
And now I dream
About Christ
Of the entire
Cosmic Snow Globe

Selah

Part 3

Christ in Unsuspecting Places

Dylan DeMarsico

I

A Fall into Grace

I AM A RECOVERING SHAME ADDICT. At the time of this writing, I'm 35 years old and the first 33 of those years were a constant war against condemnation, guilt, and a general sense of discomfort in my own skin. The difficult conclusion I have come to is how much these issues were amplified—*if not sourced*—by theological beliefs.

Ok. I'm not saying that "theology" was in the forefront of my mind guiding my developing behavior and emotions. It wasn't like someone was reading me excerpts of St. Augustine as I put on my backpack in the mornings. No one was shouting the words of John Calvin into my ears as I ate my peanut butter and jelly sandwiches at the lunch table. I'm talking about something that went much deeper than a conscious awareness of religious ideas. It was something that gets passed on through a wide variety of means, often in the subtlest of ways. It's something like an invisible web woven through every part of society, entwining with our minds and sticking to our hands.

The major theological area that contributed to this shame and discomfort involves the famous idea of "original sin." Now, we're not going to throw out that term today. I would like to just point out some poisonous implications and assumptions that often come with it. Whether intentionally or not, this concept communicates that our "origin" is sin, which is clearly not the case. (For those good at math, Genesis 1 comes before Genesis 3, when sin entered the picture.)

The idea is often communicated like this: *All of us are born wretched sinners at heart. To the core, we are bad and corrupted.* I know for sure this was passed onto me subconsciously in a variety of forms. It then blended in with that underlying sense of condemnation, and it led to this constant feeling that I *needed* something—something to make me feel better. So, I would go from hobby to hobby, chasing the next thing to try and find some sense of belonging and satisfaction. Some would call this an "addictive personality," and it led to quite a bit of unhealthy habits and behaviors.

When I was 20 years old, I surrendered my life to Jesus and became a Christian. Even though my life was transformed in many ways, this pattern of discomfort continued to affect me. The initial season of awakening to Christ brought satisfaction and love; however, there were other elements keeping me in this cycle of shame. What I've come to see is how the lack of clarity about our original design is a big part of the problem.

This lack of clarity mixed with that ongoing sense of shame made room for me to continue chasing after the next thing. The only difference was now it was "Christian" things I was chasing after. I chased revival, experiences, a stage, a cool new revelation. Peace, joy, and love would come in spurts, but never remain. I would always resort back to this cycle of feeling uncomfortable and guilty and in need of something. But toward the end of my 33rd year, something in me shifted. I find it significant that this happened at this particular point in my life. Historically, it is believed that Jesus died at age 33. Similarly, my 33rd year felt like a death.

During the Covid pandemic, I started driving a truck at night. Every evening I would be alone for hours on end, and in that place I was forced to face this lifelong battle with shame head on. After 13 years of being a Christian, I was frustrated that I was still having these issues, and yet I knew it was God's will for me to be totally free from this inner war. I knew there was a real place where striving ceased.

And so, I took a fall.

A fall into grace.

In that moment, and in a handful of other moments in the weeks and months that followed (including a deep dive *Into the Abyss*, a book by Mo Thomas, who you just heard from), I began to accept the grace of God that always existed in my life. And here was the truly groundbreaking part of all this: Through the eyes of the Holy Spirit, I saw how God created me in my mother's womb, and that I was created good—in God's image—without need of anything other than what was already inside of me.

Because of this, I read the first chapter of John many times during that season:

> *All things came into being through Him, and apart from Him nothing came into being that has come into being. In Him was life, and the life was the Light of men.*
> *~ John 1:3-4*

Jesus showed me that my very being was made through him, and that I've never existed apart from him. This began to give me a deep sense of value. I saw myself as a baby that Christ had infused with his being and imprint. God began to show me that my whole life I'd been striving for the value I already had.

My human body, my personality, my spirit—my overall being—it came from Christ, the One who made all things and therefore made me (Colossians 1:16-17). With this realization, the shame, guilt, and striving began to be silenced in my life. God was developing a deeper center in me. In a very real, God made me. I'm not a mistake or deformed. I'm fearfully and wonderfully made.

The veil was torn from my eyes and I began to see clearly. I saw that when Jesus said to *"become like little children"* he was telling me to be restored to the childhood innocence I had lost along the way (Matthew 18:3). The false belief that I was inherently a mistake, which manifested in a life of sin, distorted my childhood and took away my purity and innocence of heart. But now Christ was removing the veil over my life, and I was seeing God's glory afresh.

At 20 years old I had said "yes" to Jesus, to following his ways—this was my "salvation moment" when the power of God transformed me from the inside out. But that's not to say Jesus wasn't already present in my life beforehand! After all, he is omnipresent, which means he's everywhere. This means something! Jesus had always been there, even if it was in a *hidden* way. *"In him was life, and the life was the light of all people,"* John writes. This included me, from the moment I was born. The light of my entire life was Christ. Anything good that ever happened to me, through me, for me, was through the light of Jesus Christ.

So, what about the evil in my life?

Well, that came in because of what we might call an "original lie."

Much of the evil that ever happened in my life was because I was deceived by this world system and by very real influences of darkness enticing me to go after things that I never needed. Yes, I fell into sin. As the Scriptures say, *"We have all fallen short of the glory of God"* (Romans 3:23). This sin was a horrible problem in need of deep forgiveness and cleansing. But that was exactly what Christ had already done at the cross. He had already died to forgive me. Now he was freely restoring me and showing me my true identity in him!

With this, I realized that Christ was always the mystery hidden within me, from birth, and it was just a matter of time before I was awakened to him by faith!

> *To whom God willed to make known what is the riches of the glory of this mystery among the Gentiles, which is Christ in you, the hope of glory.*
> *~ Colossians 1:27*

Paul says the mystery of the gospel is the message of Christ in you . . .

It's important to know that when Paul says, "the glory of this mystery among the Gentiles," the word for "among" is actually the same Greek word used for "in" in the next part of the sentence ("which is Christ *in* you . . ."). In other words, Paul is saying, "The glory of this mystery *in* the Gentiles (the godless nations) . . . which is Christ *in* you."

In other words, the mystery is there already, waiting to be discovered!

This reality is true for every human being who's ever existed. There is no existence apart from Christ. All things live and move and have their being in him (see Acts 17:28 and Colossians 1:16-17). Human beings have become addicted to anything and everything because they are blinded to the truth—the truth that their existence is intertwined with the being of Christ. It is because of this reality that we have immeasurable value.

We have spent most, if not all, of human history chasing after things we don't need. The good news is that we can simply fall into grace. We can let the lies of the enemy fall off of us. We come from a good God who created us as his good children. We just need to wake up to the truth so that our lives will begin to align with it.

This is called *faith*.

II

A Tale of Two Psalms

Let's delve a little further into this topic of original sin. As we just said, the key idea behind this doctrine is that we are "born sinners." This doesn't just mean a propensity to practice sinful things. It means that from the moment we are conceived, at our core, we are sinners. In other words, our very identity is depraved.

Now there's a lot more nuance and theological depth I'm not covering here. Many people would come in and disagree and put clarifications and footnotes to the above paragraph. I'll let the scholars and social media warriors argue over the fine print. I'm just trying to deal with what gets communicated and received by the everyday person, even in popular culture.

For example, in the world of hip-hop you'll find some well-known songs carrying this general concept. A famous rapper named J Cole has an album called *"Born Sinner"* and Notorious B.I.G. says this of himself in his hit song Juicy:

"Born sinner, the opposite of a winner."

This belief that we are born as sinners to the core has become so common in our society that to question it is to question a sacred idol. But that is exactly what I'm doing here, knowing full well that I may be accused of false teaching. Yet I am going to proceed, because of how much confusion and bondage these ideas can lead to.

So where does this teaching come from? It stems from many places, but one of the key go-to verses for this doctrine is from another song, one much older than Juicy. It's from one of the top hits in a catalog of music that was popular during the days of ancient Israel. You know it as the book of Psalms:

> *Behold, I was brought forth in iniquity,*
> *And in sin my mother conceived me.*
>   ~ Psalm 51:5

King David is the author of this verse, and the context is from when he was in a deep state of repentance. After having slept with another man's wife (and then going on to arrange the murder of that individual), David was filled with a horrifying awareness of his own brokenness. In that place, David makes this remark that his mother conceived him in sin.

Many people use this verse to back up this larger theological idea of original sin; however, there is a more biblically sound way of interpreting these lyrics.

Over the centuries, rabbis and scholars have suggested that David himself was the result of an affair. We won't go into all the details here, but there is great evidence that Jesse, the father of David, had his son out of wedlock.

Many see this as the underlying reason as to why David was not invited to the feast where Samuel wanted to anoint one of Jesse's sons as king (1 Samuel 16). Jesse did not let Samuel know about David, claiming that it was because David was the "youngest." However, there is evidence in the Bible suggesting David was not the youngest of Jesse's sons (compare 1 Chronicles 2:13-15 with 1 Samuel 16:10-11). Jesse also said David was busy taking care of the sheep and thus unable to attend the feast. Yet we learn in the next chapter that there were plenty of servants available to take his place in shepherding.

In all likelihood, David's existence as Jesse's son was either covered up or minimized until the day Samuel arrived and forced Jesse to publicly acknowledge him. It makes sense then that David was rejected and hated by his half-brothers (1 Samuel 17:28). As the black sheep in the family, David knew what it was like to battle with the spirit of rejection.

Amazingly, this same spirit is exactly what David's divine descendent, Jesus Christ, came to conquer. Jesus, the son of David, would have grown up under a very similar scorn from unbelieving neighbors and extended family.

No one would have believed Mary was actually impregnated by Yahweh himself.

Everyone probably believed it was from a pre-marital affair or some other scandalous reason. As a result, David was more a foreshadow of Jesus than we realize. Even though Jesus wasn't born from an actual affair, he experienced the same weight of rejection as his kingly ancestor, and he bore this pain as part of his vicarious work on our behalf.

All this to say that when David wrote that he was "born into iniquity," he was probably talking about a pattern of sexual sin in his family line.

Now, whether you believe that interpretation or not, we still have to reckon with something else David wrote in another one of his other songs. Look at what David sings out in Psalm 71:

> *From birth I have relied on you;*
> *You brought me forth from my mother's womb.*
> *I will ever praise you.*
>   *~ **Psalm 71:6** (**NIV**)*

In this Psalm, David says the total opposite of what is suggested in Psalm 51. Here, David states that he was born relying on God. Another translation says, "Upon you I have leaned from before my birth" (Psalm 71:6 ESV).

Why doesn't someone read this passage and create a doctrine called "original lean?" Or "original relying?" Does every baby come out of their mother's wombs leaning and relying on God, simply because David said it once in the Psalms?

The real point here is that it's ridiculous to assume every single child is born as a sinner because David had a low moment in Psalm 51 after doing something terrible. In another Psalm he says he was born relying on God, which shows that we can't cherry pick single verses and create a whole doctrine around them.

All Have Sinned

Of course, there's another key passage used for this teaching.

> *For all have sinned and fall short of the glory of God.*
> *~ Romans 3:23*

Let's make something clear as we go forward and unpack this more. Sin is real. Evil is real. Everyone *has* participated in it. It doesn't take a rocket scientist to figure that out. As a whole, the Scriptures communicate that all have strayed into darkness and fallen short of the glory of God.

But let's think about this logically for a second. How can we fall short of something if we weren't created to be it in the first place? The fact that when we sin, we fall short of the glory of God implies that we were created *with* the glory of God. In other words, God has crowned human beings with his glory (which is from another one of David's chart-topping Tabernacle hits in Psalm 8). Because of this reality, when someone sins, they are falling short of the glory that is already upon them.

And consider this: If Christ *is* the full glory of God (see 2 Corinthians 4:4 & Hebrew 1:3), then we are falling short of *the Christ* that is upon us. (You might have to read that again.)

So let's be even clearer: Falling into sin isn't the same thing as believing it to be your very identity. I think the enemy of our souls would love nothing more than to have every last human being on the planet believe they are sinners at their core. This is truly the devil's plan—to confuse our identity. But God's plan is to convince us of *his identity for us*. And this is the central work of the Holy Spirit in the New Testament:

> *The Spirit Himself testifies with our spirit that we are children of God.*
> *~ Romans 8:16*

The Spirit is here to convince us of the truth—that we are God's children (see John 16:13). It's in this convincing that we begin to live out the truth in our lives.

Remember this simple and obvious reality: The devil can't create people. The devil has never, not once, ever in the history of humanity created one single soul. Psalm 139—yet another hit from Notorious King David—rings true for every human being who's ever existed:

> *For You formed my inward parts;*
> *You wove me in my mother's womb.*
> *I will give thanks to You, for I am fearfully and wonderfully made;*
> *Wonderful are Your works,*
> *And my soul knows it very well.*
> ~ **Psalm 139:13-14**

God creates beautiful and wondrous things. And that's exactly what happened when he made you in your mom's tummy. David's Bathsheba moment cannot outweigh the fact that God is gloriously good, and he creates gloriously good things. And this is still true with every person born after Adam's original act of sin.

The Bible says that *"in Adam all die"* (see 1 Corinthians 15:22 & Romans 5:12-21). This is another key verse that surrounds these theological concepts. It reminds us that every person does indeed experience death as they fall for the same lie as Adam and Eve. *But let's consider that lie for a moment.* Essentially, the devil tricked Eve into believing she was missing something. Think about the story. Eve was tempted to eat from the forbidden tree because the serpent told her she would become "like God" if she did so. But we know from Genesis 1 that she was already made in "the likeness of God!" Eve fell for a lie about her core identity, which led to a breakdown in her behavior and actions.

The devil tried the same trick with Jesus, the One who is called the "Last Adam" (1 Corinthians 15:45). In the wilderness, the enemy tried to get Jesus to trespass by subtly throwing doubt into his identity: *"If you are the Son of God…"* (Matthew 4:3). The point here is that sin comes from believing a lie. Therefore, the "original sin" is really about deception.

Problematic and "trespassing" behavior follows the distortion of our identity. Even though people are indeed born into a world where sin and death creeps into their lives easily and quickly, it is not who they are. And, again, it is this very lie that propagates

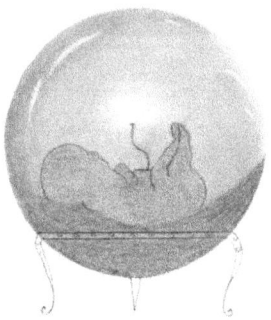

sin in the first place. This is why we pick up our cross and follow Jesus as he calls us into our new and true identity in him.

Truth Bomb

Let the truth of God hit your heart and set you free. You can end your rat race. You don't have an "addictive personality." You were just deceived as a child, just like the rest of us. You were convinced through a million different ways, whether it was words from a parent, a sibling, actions from a co-worker or a teacher, or simply the pursuit of desires ignited by television and marketing—you were sold the lie that you were missing something, that you were born with some sort of deformity, and that you need to find something to fix it. This idea of a broken identity is the very thing that has kept you in this elusive pursuit of something you can never seem to find.

Lies, lies, lies, all lies. And it comes from worldly ideas and philosophies that have infiltrated well-meaning church teachings over the centuries. But none of that changes the fact that God intimately molded and designed you in your mom's belly. He knew exactly what he was doing. He gave you the very nature, light, and shared being of Christ (check out John 1 again).

You've always been *"altogether lovely"* to him (Song of Songs 4:7). He was always there. Every good thing, every bit of love, joy, and peace you've ever experienced. It was him. All him. And he doesn't condemn you for becoming deceived. He forgives you and continues to call you to wake up to the glory that's always been hiding inside of you, waiting to come alive.

You weren't created by the devil. You weren't created *inherently evil*. Yes, you've sinned, but it was only because you've been tricked to go after other things.

You were created by God. You have value. You've always had value. He's been hiding in your life this entire time. And now you're waking up.

III

The Circumcision of Christ

A question, in light of the above . . . How are we to understand "salvation" in Christ?

Before we try to answer this, it's important to remember that salvation is meant to be experienced more than understood. As Proverbs 3:5 reads, *"Trust in the Lord with all your heart, and do not lean on your own understanding."* We are to partake of the body and blood of Christ, fellowship with his sweet presence, and simply abide and rest in who he is as our Savior.

That being said, God has given us the mind of Christ. He calls us to think healthy, biblical thoughts. At some point, we can begin to reflect on the wonderful salvation we've received and hopefully gain a life-giving understanding of it.

Most people, myself included, typically understand salvation in the "new creation" sense. Among other Scriptures, this comes from the words of 2 Corinthians 5:17, which tells us, *"The old is gone and the new has come. If anyone is in Christ, he is a new creation."* This is the main and simple way of understanding what Christ does for us. *"I once was lost, but now I'm found,"* the classic hymn goes. If I could sum up this understanding of salvation with one word, it would be this:

Transformation.

But I'd like to offer another way of seeing salvation, a way I believe is also biblical. I need to stress to you, the reader, that this does not replace the "transformation" understanding. 2 Corinthians 5:17 isn't going anywhere. But I would like to offer something that brings more depth to our understanding, especially in view of this reality of humanity's true identity. In order to do this, we have to talk about a practice called circumcision.

An Embarassing Question

I'm going to confess something pretty funny to you—and slightly embarrassing. At 34 years old, I realized that I wasn't one hundred percent sure if I was circumcised or not. I had a moment of confusion. Wait, what exactly is circumcision? Am I circumcised? Do only Jewish people get circumcised? I'm not Jewish, does that mean I'm uncircumcised?

Now we can probably blame my mom and dad a little bit for never explaining this to me, or maybe my health teacher. But I think most of the blame should go to me for never paying attention that much to my mom, dad, or the health teacher. I wasn't very teachable for most of my life. And so I awkwardly, yet hilariously, confessed this to my dear friend and co-author, Nick Padovani.

We laughed for a while, made fun of me, and cracked jokes. We found a very professional illustrated picture of the difference between an uncircumcised and circumcised penis. The Holy Spirit had to persuade me to not use that picture for this book in an effort to avoid any silly controversy . . . or at least a word from my wife. *Uh, Dylan, what did you and Nick just send to my email?*

And so, I finally arrived at an answer to this lifelong quagmire. I, Dylan DeMarsico, was in fact circumcised. *Phewph*, what a relief! For a few days I thought I might be outside of the people of God. Praise the Lord, I was snipped at infancy, like most modern male children, I think.

If you are like me, and you actually need a basic understanding of circumcision, let me give you a quick rundown. When a male child is born, they are born with an elongated piece of foreskin that covers the tip of the penis. If, like me, you need a visual representation, do an image search for "circumcised penis" and you will get a bunch of nice, illustrated pictures that explain it all. Just make sure to delete your browser history after that. Just kidding. Once Nick and I stopped laughing, we actually realized something pretty amazing about salvation…

A few times in the New Testament, salvation is compared to circumcision. Most notably, to me at least, is Romans 2:29.

> *But he is a Jew who is one inwardly; and circumcision is that which is of the heart, by the Spirit, not by the letter; and his praise is not from men, but from God.*
> *~ Romans 2:29*

There's also Colossians 2:11:

> *And in Him you were also circumcised with a circumcision made without hands, in the removal of the body of the flesh by the circumcision of Christ.*
> *~ Colossians 2:11*

Even in the Old Testament, there was a hint of this through the prophet Jeremiah. It reads:

> *Circumcise yourselves to the Lord and remove the foreskin of your heart.*
> *~ Jeremiah 4:4*

Jeremiah prophesied a time when the people of God would have the foreskin of their hearts removed. Just like the foreskin is removed from males in order to reveal the head of a reproductive organ, the foreskin of our hearts is removed in order to reveal something that was already there—in our case, a heart made in the image of God!

Okay. Did you catch all that? Let me slow down and explain a little more. Earlier, I gave the one word I would use to describe our typical Christian understanding of salvation. That word was *"transformation."* If I could pick one word to describe this circumcision understanding of salvation, it would be this:

Revealing.

The gospel transforms us and *reveals* something within us that was hidden all along behind an "extra layer of skin"—metaphorically speaking. In circumcision, the removal of the foreskin reveals the part of the male organ that releases *life*—literally speaking. The question then is, what is revealed when Christ removes the foreskin of our hearts?

Our true heart . . . the heart that is filled with life. . . the God-kind of Life. This is the heart God so beautifully molded in our mother's womb.

This circumcision understanding of salvation could also be described like this: Your whole life you were hidden behind this extra layer of unnecessary "skin" that was blocking the real Christlike you from being revealed. Salvation is simply when Christ removes that unnecessary layer of unbelief, deception, and sin.

This is what Paul expresses throughout the book of Colossians. At the cross, Christ removed our "foreskin" and redeemed the image of God within us. The apostle calls this the *"circumcision of Christ."* He makes the point that it's not regular human hands, or a doctor's hands, that cut off our foreskin; rather it's the hands of the Son of God, delicately, yet powerfully, removing the foreskin of our hearts. Through this circumcision of heart, God restores us back to his full likeness. As it says a little later in Colossians:

> *. . . seeing that you have put off the old self with its practices and have put on the new self, which is being renewed in knowledge after the image of its Creator.*
> ~ *Colossians 3:9-10* (ESV)

Christ tells us as believers that we are to "see" (to perceive, believe, trust, remember) that we have put off the old self. If you think about it, the new self is actually older than the old self. It's the *original self* God created in the garden of Eden *"in the image of its Creator."* This is the original blessing of God that came before "original sin." And in another letter from Paul, we learn how God made up his mind about this before the foundation of the world:

> *Even as he chose us in him before the foundation of the world, that we should be holy and blameless before him.*
> ~ *Ephesians 1:4* (ESV)

Are you still with me? Let me try to wrap this up here. Maybe going from "old to new" is the same thing as going from "false to true." The spiritual foreskin we've all carried was never meant for us. I would suggest the reason God even created foreskin and circumcision is to be a parable for our salvation. We always had our true "image of God self" inside of us in a hidden way, but there was something blocking its flow. And that something has been removed by Christ. Now, as we put our trust in who he is and what he's done, our true image of God-self comes to life. We can now freely walk in who we truly are as ones made in the likeness and glory of God. He created us to be a radiant picture of his love and character, to be like him in all his ways. In other words, we are now free to live out the fruit of the Spirit: love, joy, peace, kindness, and more.

Every Good and Perfect Gift

This has the potential to change the way we see our entire lives, even going back to our childhood. For me, I struggled to see where Jesus was in my past, especially before I had accepted him. But as God has opened my eyes to these things, I've discovered he was hiding in simple yet beautiful places…

Every time my mom or dad sacrificed their time for me. Every moment somebody shared a toy or some food with me. Every instance where I took the time to love someone. Every good thing I ever did. It was only through him. Like James wrote, *"Every good gift and every perfect gift is from above, coming down from the Father of lights"* (James 1:17 ESV). Understanding that the image and likeness of God was hidden inside of me, and the people around me, even in my past, allows me to realize that God was always involved in my life.

There is something deeply refreshing and redeeming about this. And it makes me love Jesus all the more. It makes me think, *"Wow, even when I was covered in sin, and deceived by the enemy, God was still working in my life and in my heart, even if I didn't see it or know it."* It shows me that God is so much more merciful and gracious than I ever realized. God didn't only enter my life when I gave my life to his Son. He was already in my life before I surrendered. I'm so grateful for this.

Now, to say it again for the people in the back: This does not excuse sin. Sin is sin.

My spiritual foreskin had to be removed. It was only when Jesus called my name and awakened me, that the foreskin was removed—and I was saved.

There is a balance here. When Jesus hung on the cross, he was removing the foreskins of the world once and for all. At the same time, however, it is only once a person surrenders to him and gives him their heart—their foreskinned heart—that they see this darkness personally fall off in their life. *This is where the "revealing" and the "transformation" aspects of salvation come together.*

In this way, the cross seems to stand outside of time. Its power meets us where we're at, thousands of years later, when we embrace what he has done. And it's still as powerful as ever. (And I understand all of this is perhaps in line with what some people mean when they speak of how God deals with "original sin." But concepts come with baggage, and we need to purify the waters and make sure we are understanding the full meaning of the good news of Jesus. That is the hope of this writing.)

There's an interesting Old Testament shadow of this reality from the life of our good friend David. Not only was he a great songwriter, but as you probably know he was also quite the warrior. One time, David had to fetch one hundred Philistine foreskins in order to acquire his bride. Really gross. But that's what he did. He defeated the uncircumcised Philistines and brought their foreskins to the king as the dowry gift to have his daughter as a bride (1 Samuel 18:20-30).

Think about the parallels here. Jesus finds the one created to be his true bride—the human race—by removing the foreskin of deception around our hearts. He accomplished this act of warfare once and for all at the cross. And yet, at the same time, we are not forced into marriage. A true bride gives her own "yes" to her beloved.

God highly values free will. A relationship of love must go two ways. Therefore, we have to be willing to accept this wedding gift of freedom. Again, this is what makes his finished work (the work of destroying humanity's sinful false self) real and transformational in our lives.

Now this understanding of salvation brings another thing to our understanding. It changes the way we see others, and therefore the way we treat them. It brings about a revolution in how we see things like ministry and missions. This is where everything has been leading and it will take a whole other section to explore…

IV

Seeing Christ Hidden in All

Only a few days before he gave his life for the world, Jesus spoke the following words. Take a moment to read this, even if you've heard it many times before:

> *"Then the King will say to those on his right, 'Come, you who are blessed by my Father, inherit the kingdom prepared for you from the foundation of the world. For I was hungry and you gave me food, I was thirsty and you gave me drink, I was a stranger and you welcomed me, I was naked and you clothed me, I was sick and you visited me, I was in prison and you came to me.'*
>
> *Then the righteous will answer him, saying, 'Lord, when did we see you hungry and feed you, or thirsty and give you drink? And when did we see you a stranger and welcome you, or naked and clothe you? And when did we see you sick or in prison and visit you?'*
>
> *And the King will answer them, 'Truly, I say to you, as you did it to one of the least of these my brothers, you did it to me.'"*
> ~ *Matthew 25:34-40* (ESV)

In this passage, Jesus identifies himself with some questionable subjects. We can try to soften his meaning by saying he's speaking in some kind of loose metaphoric way—but what if Jesus really means what he says here? What if he really is hidden in and with every single person?

Even if we do take these words loosely, Jesus still refers to the poor, hungry, thirsty, and imprisoned as *his brothers*. There's no way around that. They are fellow members of the family of God. Thus, our kindness toward people is a kindness toward Jesus himself.

There's no way around this reality.

What if you started to truly recognize that Jesus Christ is hidden in every single person you come across. And furthermore, what if you saw the entire human race as your family? Would it change the way you treated people? Might the Holy Spirit's fruits of love, joy, and peace come about more easily and quickly? Would you have a more honorable posture toward your fellow human beings?

Obviously, there are many people living in darkness. We don't want to ignore that. We will always hold to the vision of seeing real freedom—actual righteousness—filling people's lives. But in this context, we're talking about discovering the value of every single person, and the reality that Jesus's life is intimately connected to the life of humanity.

This perspective is at the heart of the evangelism modeled by the apostle Paul. He was convinced of the reality that *"one died for all and therefore all died"* (2 Corinthians 5:14). He then connected this truth with the following statement: *"Therefore, from now on, we regard no one according to the flesh…"* (v. 16).

Paul was unable to see anyone solely through their outward human appearance. Instead, he saw the potential of Christ's overflowing life within every person. He knew their original value. Coinciding with this, Paul understood that every person had been included in that moment Jesus gave his life at the cross. The apostle John echoed the same truths when he wrote:

> *He is the atoning sacrifice for our sins, and not only for ours but also for the sins of the whole world.*
> *~ 1 John 2:2* **(NIV)**

Paul took this reality into the mission field and let it guide the way he viewed humanity. Christ had truly accomplished something for the whole world, hence his declaration at the cross: *"It is finished"* (John 19:30).

You can think about it this way: When we see the original value of Christ hidden in people who don't even know him, we are viewing them "by faith." Faith is seeing things that are unseen. It's the conviction of things hoped for (Hebrews 11:1). We see what they themselves haven't yet discovered. We are convicted that, in spite of their current situation, Christ and his love is at the core of their existence. And it's from that place that we are empowered to love them with kindness, joy, and long-suffering love (see 1 Corinthians 13:4-7). And we are called to do the same as our Father who *"calls into existence the things that do not exist"* (Romans 4:17). We speak to the potential that's hidden within and then it starts to come to life!

The Outsiders

In another one of his writings, Paul made a strong connection between faith and love: *"The only thing that counts is faith expressing itself through love"* (Galatians 5:6 NIV). When we have the faith that sees the face of Christ in everyone, love springs forth. Like Paul, it is then our joy to go to all people—even "outsiders—and share the message of *"Christ in you, the hope of the glory"* (Colossians 1:27).

Christ is always going after those who feel unloved. His compelling desire is to persuade them of his infinite love, and of the truth of who they are in his eyes. People hearing and receiving this message is how transformation and revelation breaks loose.

There are so many groups of people who feel like an outsider to God's love. One particular group of our day might be those who identify as gay, lesbian, or transgender. Many of them believe God has been cut off from them. This belief then reinforces their fear and keeps them stuck in a cycle of rejecting the love and healing of Jesus. It will be through seeing Jesus in them and loving them accordingly that they wake up to who they really are. It's God's kindness that leads people to change their lives (Romans 2:4).

This was how Christ did ministry as well. He picked those who were on the outside of what the religious leadership would deem acceptable. He picked fishermen, tax collectors, and religious zealots. The Scriptures suggest he even had a former prostitute in his inner circle. From the beginning of his ministry, Jesus told all of them, *"You are the light of the world"* (Matthew 5:14). He said this before the Holy Spirit was poured out! This is a great example of Jesus seeing the potential in people and calling it out, even while they were still struggling along in their journey.

He also called them to pray "our Father" right in the beginning of his ministry. Again, he calls them to sonship and daughterhood, even before the Holy Spirit was revealed in the book of Acts. Jesus was speaking into their destiny even if they hadn't fully realized it yet.

The parable of the prodigal son, which Jesus told to a group comprised of both religious leaders and religious outcasts, expressed all of this as well. In that story, the father of the prodigal young man never stopped believing that his son was his son—even though the son wasn't living the way he should. We can have this same heart toward people all over the world who aren't living the right way. We can believe they are truly God's children, and from that place, we can manifest a tangible love for them.

And of course, we can then be ready to party whenever these children do wake up and remember who they truly are and Whose they truly are…

> *For this son of mine was dead and has now returned to life. He was lost, but now he is found.' So <u>the party</u> began. Meanwhile, the older son was in the fields working. When he returned home, he heard <u>music and dancing in the house</u> . . .*
> ~ *Luke 15:24-25* **(NLT)**

Case Study: The Quakers & the Inner Light

As we begin to wrap up these discussions, it would be helpful to look at how these truths have tangibly changed the world, particularly through those who passionately held to this reality. One group that stands out from the rest is the Society of Friends. Or, as their detractors called them, the Quakers.

The Quakers were founded by a passionate follower of Jesus named George Fox who wrote the words, *"There is that of God in every man."* He cast a wide-angle lens at a world he believed was filled with the beauty and image of the Father. Fox still understood that people needed to come into their own relationship with God, but he treated them the same whether they had embraced this relationship or not.

This truth about the image and glory of God resting within each person became a guiding focus for many of the world-changing things the Quakers went on to engage in. And that is not an exaggeration. Few people realize the full impact the Quakers had on shaping the world we live in today. It is beyond the scope of this writing to capture everything; but suffice it to say that much of the freedoms we enjoy today are a result of the suffering love of Quakers and their fight for justice and righteousness in society.

Men and women within the Quaker community were often on the right side of history with key issues we take for granted today. The Quakers were often in direct opposition to many of the professing Christians of their day. This included their stance in how they treated women, African slaves, and indigenous communities. Filled with a fire from the Holy Spirit, this group fought for biblical justice amongst people groups that many parts of the church had resisted.

One person who was particularly influenced by the Quaker perspective was a man named William Penn, the founder of Pennsylvania and the author of governmental documents that went on to be the chief influences of the U.S. Constitution.

Compared to his contemporaries, Penn had an otherworldly relationship with the First Nations people. Because of his guiding belief of the inner light and the image of God in his Native brothers and sisters, Penn treated them with an unprecedented amount of honor and respect. And it was literally unprecedented. The people from the mostly Christianized continent of Europe did not treat the Natives the way Penn did. As a result, he garnered a deep measure of trust with them.

One notable story is when Penn enacted the Shackamaxon Treaty with the Lenape Nation in 1683. This treaty led to a brief period of peace between those who traveled from

Europe for spiritual freedom and those who were the original stewards of this "new" land. Penn set up this treaty on the basis of Fox's teachings that *there is that of God in every man*. The treaty has been described as the true "seed" of our nation.[1]

Unfortunately, not long after Penn was forced to return to Europe to deal with unrelated business, there were other leaders who rose up after him who did not share his Quaker beliefs. They went on to deceive the Native communities, breaking the treaty many times over.

It did not help that the overarching theology of the European church de-emphasized the glory and beauty of God in all people. Whether people are aware of this or not, these ideas have a way of trickling down into how we live and move in this world. George Fox was an outlier who was persecuted and derided for his beliefs. His understanding of the faith did not jive with many of the people in power. However, if others had held to his convictions (and to this larger theological framework), American history surely would have unfolded in a much different way.

Sadly, that original seed of our nation went into the ground and died. Yet we believe it is still buried there in the ground. It only waits to be watered and ignited by those who will return to the truth of God's original blessing—those who will see people the way Christ sees people, who will follow the example of William Penn and the original Quakers. There is such hope for our future if this path is recovered.

The Great Commission

Hopefully, you can see how this is bigger than wrestling over the finer points of theology. This is actually where the rubber hits the road in regard to the Great Commission. The foundation of God's love for all people leads to a beautiful way of winning hearts for the Kingdom of God. It is not done through force, domination, fear, or by any semblance of religious manipulation. It is accomplished, rather, by a people who truly see the image of God within humanity and are so compelled by the glory of this truth that they lay down their lives on behalf of their lost brothers and sisters.

---

[1] *The Seed of a Nation: Rediscovering America* by Darrell Fields. Morgan James Publishing 2008.

The Great Commission is at the heart of transforming the world. Yes, it is about reconciling people with their Maker, but it also about reconciling people with one another. This is a major reason as to why Jesus tied so many of his teachings about the Kingdom of God to the topic of forgiveness. He knew that the expansion of his Kingdom would have to be marked by a radical "letting go" of all that we hold against each other.

And this, of course, brings us right back to the words of Paul in 2 Corinthians 5 where he says that we are *"ministers of reconciliation."* Such a title changes the way we think about this subject. Missions isn't merely doing good things for people or giving them some vague understanding of cultural Christianity. Missions, at its heart, is awakening people to the glory inside of them—and inside of one another. Missions is about calling the family of God back together. It is about those with the heart of a father or mother, who go after those who feel orphaned and alone, releasing a "word" of extra-ordinary joy.

This is a deeply inspiring reason to go to another country or to a specific people group. This is what motivated Paul to travel across nations and give his life to missions. And this is the great adventure that is laid before us, whether we travel far or stay and release this truth to the people right in our own neighborhood.

The globe is filled with the snow of God's righteousness, hidden in all people and all places. We get to go and call it forth.

V

Behold, the Riddle

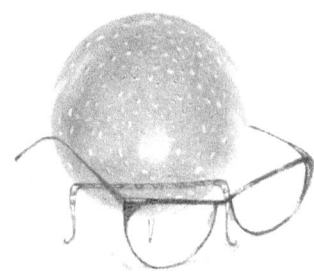

As we close this part up, let me try and recap the essence of what we just learned by looking at one more story from the Bible:

> *Jesus saw Nathanael coming to Him, and said of him, "Behold, an Israelite indeed, in whom there is no deceit!"*
>
> *Nathanael said to Him, "How do You know me?" Jesus answered and said to him, "Before Philip called you, when you were under the fig tree, I saw you."*
>
> *Nathanael answered Him, "Rabbi, You are the Son of God; You are the King of Israel."*
> ~ *John 1:47-49*

In this story, Jesus revealed that he had seen Nathanael before Nathanael saw him. This led Nathanael to a place of awe and wonder, as well as a declaration that Jesus was and is the Son of God.

This is a great example of what the revelation of the Snow Globe accomplishes in our hearts. Jesus reveals that he was in our lives before we recognized it. *He knew us before we knew him*. And because of this, we are filled with awe, wonder, and delight in the Son of God. He is truly amazing. He is involved in the lives of every human being, whether they know him yet or not.

If our understanding of salvation is only that God appears when we first believe in him, we actually miss out on how he was always pursuing us and involved in our lives even while we were in sin and doubt.

God is intimately acquainted with every human being whether they have come to their moment of salvation or not. This should make us fall more in love with God for his goodness. He doesn't leave his creation, even when it's blind to him.

God is truly everywhere. That's one of the core aspects of God's nature—his omnipresence. The best part of that term is *presence*. God is *present* and available with intention and care to every part of the world. His omnipresence isn't just his invisible "force" side. **It's him!** It's his heart and fullness—in all, with all, and through all (1 Corinthians 8:6).

My life's mission is to know this God . . . to *"progressively become more deeply and intimately acquainted with him, perceiving and recognizing and understanding the wonders of His Person more strongly and more clearly"* (Philippians 3:10 AMPC). All this revelation about his loving omnipresence is simply another way I've discovered him. (Or, to say it more accurately, a way in which he's revealed himself to me.) And it helps me to see people the way God sees them, even in their struggle.

Calling Out the Gold

Many of us have heard the phrase before: *"Call out the gold in people."* Some of the men and women that impacted me the most have done just that. It leaves a deep mark in your life when someone chooses to see beyond your baggage—behind the "uncircumcised foreskin" that everyone else focuses on.

I know most Christians who have experienced the love of Jesus tend to treat people this way. Yet I also know, from experience, that there is always a temptation to see people for who they're not. Calling out sin and correcting people is vital in the kingdom, but we need to do it with the person's true potential in mind. This is why we need these truths about God's loving omnipresence as well as this revelation of the "snow" that covers and fills the globe. This leads us to remember people's true hearts. It helps us see beyond the "foreskin" they may be under.

We leave here, then, with a call to look deep within our neighbor and to see the image and likeness of God within . . . to call people out of their false identities . . . to invite them to reach out and reconnect with the One who has already reconciled himself with all creation. For the omnipresent One still longs to be invited in. That is indeed the only way transformation comes.

We want to make this so very clear. Even with this renewed vision of creation and humanity, there is still an urgent call for people to wake up and turn from darkness. Every believer is given a sacred charge to invite people higher, and to bring correction with grace and patience as the Spirit of the Creator leads. The motivation of this always comes back to the gold inside. We see the precious and pure diamond their heart really is, which requires ongoing patience and love.

Thank God, those are the very things Christ has given us. So, let's love the world. Let's love the "worst of the worst." The addicts, the prostitutes, the alcoholics, the porn addicts. Everyone the world deems as failures. Like Christ who saw the potential within his earliest followers, let's love people and care for them, over long periods of time, without giving up on them, even if they give up on us. Let's call them into their true identity as God sees them, and teach them to follow Jesus in every way.

The Riddle Solved

With that, we'll end where we began. At the start of this volume, we connected 1 Corinthians 13 with the beautiful mystery of how God sees all creation. In the King James Version we read that when we look at life and the world we see through "a glass darkly." However, the real Greek word is the same term used for *riddles*. A riddle is something where an answer is right in front of you and yet it's wrapped up in a shroud of mystery.

> *For now we see but **a faint reflection of riddles** and mysteries as though reflected in a mirror, but one day we will see face-to-face. My understanding is incomplete now, but one day I will understand everything, just as everything about me has been fully understood.*
> ~ 1 Corinthians 13:12 **(TPT)**

Everything in our journey has led us to unveiling of this mystery.

And so, behold, the riddle of creation . . .

Behind the beggar is a king.

Behind the prostitute, a bride.

The unlocking of this riddle means that in the garbage dumps of Southeast Asia, where people live in unimaginable poverty, there are diamonds underneath the ash heaps and treasures of untold beauty waiting to be discovered.

It means that in the concrete walls of our inner cities there is incalculable glory.

In the richer parts of the world, from Wall Street to the American suburbs, an innocence has been wrapped up and preserved in the grace of Christ. Glory is there as well.

It means that in the empty, broken, and divorced households of our nations there is still a harmony resident in the souls of those affected, reaching out and inviting us to reconnect with its healing hum.

It means that in every place of worship, glory is waiting to be uncovered through a deeper revelation of Christ and his finished work. Even in dying and religious churches there is glory and innocence to be awakened.

And what is the glory of God?

It's his rich goodness. It's his truth and his grace.

Ultimately, it's Jesus Christ. Christ is the Truth about creation, because all creation is summed up in him (Ephesians 1:10).

The glory of Christ fills everything (Isaiah 6:3), and we are called to be treasure hunters who have sold everything in order to take hold of this pearl of great price—a pearl that is hidden throughout the entire field of humanity (even "animals and atoms"). The love of Christ now compels us because we have come to the most stunning conclusion:

. . . One died for all

Therefore, all died . . .

The call is to believe. And out of that joyful belief, to go and boldly share this truth with the world. For without faith, we will not access this rich inheritance. This is what the apostle Paul wrote about in the 10th chapter of Romans:

> *So then faith eliminates the distinction between Jew and non-Jew, for he is the same Lord for all people. And he has enough treasures to lavish generously upon all who call on him. And it's true: "Everyone who calls on the Lord's name will experience new life."*
> *~ Romans 10:12-13* **(TPT)**

A true faith and awareness of this message brings about that glorious experience of new life in Christ. It also breaks down the many walls erected throughout humanity. So with that, Paul goes on to make this other famous point:

> *But how can people call on him for help if they've not yet believed? And how can they believe in one they've not yet heard of? And how can they hear the message of life if there is no one there to proclaim it? And how can the message be proclaimed if messengers have yet to be sent? That's why the Scriptures say:*
> *How welcome is the arrival*
> *of those proclaiming the joyful news of peace*
> *and of good things to come!*
> *~ Romans 10:14-15* **(TPT)**

With that, we pray a release of a fiery boldness within your own heart to go and bring this message to the nations. It's wonderful to know theological truths, but it's a whole other thing to see that truth break through the soil of people's heart, resulting in true transformation in their lives and relationships ...

... and in light of the above, we desire so deeply that this little book wouldn't just be about a bunch of theological truths. We want to take this further and share some practical ways to implement and share these realities with others.

The following are two resources that can immediately help with this.

FIRST, we have a seven-part discovery series called *Awake: The Seven Facets*.

These are seven teachings that go through the message of the diamond within and how Christ came to recover our true selves. This is something that can be shared with family, friends, and neighbors. It can be shared one-on-one with someone or utilized in a group setting. You can also go through it yourself to become more grounded in the truths of original blessing, identity, and grace.

LEARN MORE AT WWW.ALMONDBRANCH.CHURCH/AWAKE

SECOND, we have a publication and media ministry called *Elisha's Riddle* that exists solely for the purpose of celebrating and unlocking this wonderful mystery of Christ.

All of us need a steady dose of truth-filled nourishment that is free from legalism and fear. For this reason, *Elisha's Riddle* puts out resources to help people stay awake to the beauty and power of the good news while also giving prophetic perspective on things happening across the world and in the larger body of Christ.

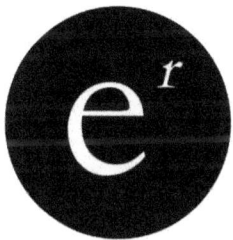

Many people contribute to this by sharing articles, artwork, and other forms of media that help others awaken even more to this glorious message of our union with God. We also have a weekly *Elisha's Riddle Podcast*.

A subscription to *Elisha's Riddle* provides support to those who are on the ground doing the good work of sharing the message of grace.

LEARN MORE AT ELISHASRIDDLE.COM

The Authors & the Press

NICK PADOVANI

Nick is a husband, a father, a social worker, and a friend of Jesus. He is also the pastor of a beautiful and flourishing church in northern New Jersey—The Almond Branch. Nick is the author of *The Song of the Ages* series. It is his joy and passion to see God's children awaken to their full inheritance in the love of Christ.

MO THOMAS

Mo is the author of *Into the Abyss: Discover Your True Identity in the Infinite Depths of Christ*. He is currently working as a STEM consultant in the education sector, helping children discover the way God sees and feels about them as they learn creative ways to explore and connect with their world. He finds his inspiration from nature and the world of science, the theological musings of the ancients, and poetry from authors like Dr. Seuss, E.E. Cummings, Mary Oliver and Rumi.

DYLAN DEMARSICO

Dylan is the co-founder of Elisha's Riddle as well as the author of *The Happy Trinity* and other works. He holds a Master of Divinity Degree from Liberty University. He and his wife Whitney focus on restoring indviduals and families through social work, children's ministry, and foster care. They currently live in Stockton, California.

You can find each of their books and much more at Eyes Open Press.

Eyes Open Press exists to spread the message of grace, identity, and freedom in Christ. Our books and media serve as a resource for spiritual awakening. We help those with a similar vision to design, edit, and professionally publish their work.

LEARN MORE AT EYESOPENPRESS.COM

"Look harder."
  ~ Rafiki